Dream FISHING
The World's Greatest Waters

Dream FISHING

The World's Greatest Waters

Trevor Housby

BLANDFORD PRESS
POOLE · NEW YORK · SYDNEY

Series Editor: Jonathan Grimwood
First published in the UK 1986 by Blandford Press
Link House, West Street, Poole, Dorset BH15 1LL

Distributed in the United States by
Sterling Publishing Co, Inc,
2 Park Avenue, New York, NY 10016

Distributed in Australia by
Capricorn Link (Australia) Pty Ltd
PO Box 665, Lane Cove, NSW 2066

British Library Cataloguing in Publication Data

Housby, Trevor
  Dream fishing: a guide to the world's
  greatest waters.
  1. Fishing
  I. Title
  799.1′2   SH439

ISBN 0 7137 16541

Typeset by Asco Trade Typesetting Ltd., Hong Kong
Printed in Spain
by Graficromo S. A.

To Bob, Josie, John and Marie Ablanalp of Walker's Cay
To Peter Kreindler of 21 Club, New York
To Francisco Van Uden of San Miguel and the people of the nine islands of
the Azores and finally
To Russell Housby, a boy, a joy, and hopefully a better angler than his
father.

Contents

Francisco Van Uden at Pescatur with a catch of nine big eye tuna, all taken on Kona Head off San Miguel, Azores. The colour used for the Kona Head should match the target species. Big eye usually prefer red and white lures, although green and yellow lures can be successful.

Introduction

Compiling an anglers' dream book has not been easy—limitations of space have meant that I have had to sift through a lifetime of angling experiences to decide on those of most importance to me. I wish I could have written more, but I would have needed 10,000 pages to record all the experiences, in waters near and far, that have given me both pleasure and good fishing. In those extra pages I could have taken my reader to many more beautiful, exciting or exotic locations, could have asked him to fish beside me for trout in the lakes of England and Canada, enjoy with me the tranquillity of giant carp on lily-girt pools and listen with me to the great splash of giant big-game fish surfacing on the oceans from New Zealand to Nova Scotia.

As it is, I have tried to share with my reader those memories that mean most to me and seem to fall within both the areas of *dream* and *greatest*. For I have been fortunate. I have been able to turn many of my boyhood dreams into adult reality. I have achieved much in a lifetime of angling—best of all, a son. Perhaps his dreams may be fired by the stories in this book. Perhaps, too, I may be granted the privilege of standing beside my son when *his* childhood dreams of angling in their turn become reality.

★ ★ ★

The choice of tackle—what rod for which species, with what reel and line— has been dealt with in detail many times before: not least in my *Big-Game Fishing* and *Trout Fishing* (both Blandford Press). Because of this, and because it is normally easier—unless you are totally fanatic—to hire the necessary equipment when you arrive at one of the world's great waters, I have not in- cluded a section on buying tackle for each of the areas or species covered within the chapters.

It is far better to try first and decide if you want to continue with that branch of our sport, before laying out largish sums of money for tackle which would be better spent on the petrol, train ticket or air fare needed to get you to where the fish are.

Good fishing.

Trevor Housby

1

Tournament Time

Battling the Big Fish

The telephone rang. On the line was Penny Taylor, who ran the Bahamas Tourist Office in London.

'I've just come back from the Bahamas,' she said, 'and guess what? I caught a white marlin from a place called Walker's Cay!'

I began to congratulate her, but she interrupted me. 'What are you doing on Friday?' she asked.

It was now Wednesday. 'Nothing,' I replied, thinking that she was planning a celebratory lunch or drink.

'In that case, how would you like to fly out to the Bahamas and compete in the Walker's Cay Billfish Tournament?'

I couldn't believe that she was serious; it seemed far too good to be true. First of all, the Bahamas are a fisherman's paradise—Ernest Hemingway fished them, and so did Kaplan, Farrington and many other legendary American anglers. Secondly, Walker's Cay was the most exciting fishing base in the whole area. It had been on the big-game fishing maps since the 1930s, but recently vast amounts of money had been poured into it to make it a dream world for the seeker of big fish. Finally, the competition in which I had been invited to take part was the most prestigious fishing tournament in the world; it attracts the best (and the richest!) anglers from every nation. The winner automatically goes into the top ten in the world's game-fishing ratings.

But Penny meant every word. She had already completed the arrangements for the trip, knowing that I would jump at the opportunity.

And so it was that two days later, on Friday morning, I left a cold, damp London on my way to the 1979 Billfish Tournament. Ten hours later, in the heat of evening, I landed at Nassau on New Providence Island. At 5 o'clock on the following morning I was back at Nassau airport to join an early flight to Freeport on Grand Bahama Island. From Freeport a two-seater plane flew me the 50 miles to Walker's Cay. As we flew over the great Bahama flats, we saw beneath us the dark shapes of large shark and ray clearly silhouetted against the white coral sands. Then we came in to land on Walker's Cay airstrip and I saw how small the island was—how small, and how beautiful, with its landscaped gardens and its magnificent beaches. It has a select marina, a luxury hotel and a club, one of whose features is a gourmet restaurant where the best of Bahamian foods are served nightly. When I arrived the owner, Bob Ablanalp, was in

Rock star Roger Daltrey fishing for blue marlin in a tournament off Walker's Cay.

New York, but the manager, David O'Shaugnessy, was on hand to show me round and introduce me to my tournament partner, Joe Pizzuro.

We were to fish from Bob's boat, *Sea Lion II*, a magnificent custom-built sport-fishing craft which featured air conditioning, ice makers, showers, and a galley equipped with a microwave and every other conceivable gadget. We had two days to go before the tournament started and we used the time to take the boat out and wet some lures. I caught several fine wahoo. The island was filling up meanwhile with contestants, owners and crews—that year 76 boats had entered the tournament. Finally the great day dawned and at half past seven we headed out to our station. To see so many superb game-fish boats racing out to sea at 25 to 30 knots was a sight I shall never forget. Doug Lindley, skipper of *Sea Lion II*, had earmarked our fishing area. He had been

Tournament angler John Ablanalp with a beautiful sailfish.

baits

boat

A livebait trolled around a basking blue marlin can be very effective. If using a deadbait, this should be trolled slightly faster.

the winning skipper in the previous year, so was a hot favourite to find fish again for this tournament.

Start time was half past eight. Out went the lines. We started to troll using Kona Head lures on the flat lines and natural baits fished far back on the outriggers. The tournament is fished on a total-weight basis; billfish are all lumped together; separate trophies are awarded for tuna, wahoo and other species. On that first day we caught one fish—a 60-pound white marlin that fell to Joe's rod. It put us in the contest but hardly among the leaders—several fish of over 200 pounds had been taken by other boats. On the second day, we saw not a single fish—but, fortunately, neither did most of the other competitors. On the third day the weather was too rough for successful trolling and very little was caught—although one contestant boated, after a four-hour battle, a blue-fin tuna that weighed in at almost 700 pounds.

John and Bob Ablanalp with heavyweight Penn 80 Class reels and rigs for tournament fishing.

A 90 lb wahoo taken during a tournament at Walker's Cay, Abaco Islands, Bahamas. Although the wahoo runs to around 100 lb in the Canary Islands and in Madeira, where it is called Cavala da India *(Indian Mackerel), it only rarely runs to 90 lb in the Bahamas.*

The weather cleared on the fourth day and every competing angler was eager to take the opportunity to get himself a big fish—the top weight had so far been on the low side and the tournament was at this stage wide open. I was a little despondent—I was not expecting to win but to have not one billfish to my credit made me feel that luck was really running against me. We set out that day towards an area we had not fished before and by midday were miles

Landing the author's prize-winning 561 lb fish, reeled in on an 80 class International reel and caught on a Kona Head lure. The fish measured 12 feet and took 40 minutes to boat.

A line of boats on just one of the docks at Walker's Cay during the annual tournament.

Author with his prize-winning blue marlin. Blue marlin are found and fished from the Caribbean to the Atlantic Islands; and have very occasionally been found as far north as Norway!

from the island and miles, too, from our nearest competitor. Some boats had sailed more than fifty miles, to a hotspot called Matanilla Reef, in the hope of fish; we had taken a chance and gone the other way.

I have to explain at this point that I come from a part of England where there is a fervently held fisherman's superstition that it is very bad luck indeed to mention the word 'rabbit' on a boat. You can talk about 'little furry things with long ears' but you cannot say 'rabbit'. I, semi-seriously, half believe that

Showing the bite taken by a tiger shark from Roger Daltrey's black fin tuna, Bahamas.

A beautiful 105 lb white marlin for the author, taken off the Abaco Islands. Marlin are also sometimes found off Madeira, the Canaries and the Azores.

there is something in this particular superstition. I used to fish with a farmer friend who would, on every trip, speak the dreaded word. In three years I never saw him catch a decent fish. You can imagine, then, my feeling when Joe appeared from the stateroom talking loudly about a rabbit shoot that he had been on. Soon afterwards he complained of a headache and retired to rest, telling me that all four rods were now mine to fish with.

Minutes later a huge marlin surfaced, passed through the natural baits we had out and headed straight for a big yellow Kona Head. To encourage it to feed I cranked the rod handle a couple of times to make the lure move faster. The fish nailed the lure solidly—it was so close that I could watch the bait vanishing into its mouth. Striking to set the hooks, I slipped straight into the

fighting chair as the fish began to crash about all over the surface. Bearing in mind that Joe had jinxed the boat with that word 'rabbit', I expected the fish to fall off at any second. But no. I fought it hard on the 80-pound class outfit and 40 minutes later brought it into the gaff. The crew went mad with excitement as the fish slid in through the tuna door in *Sea Lion*'s transom. It was so huge that it was obvious at that moment that we had the contest in the bag. At the weigh-in that afternoon I watched as the marlin registered on the beam scales at a fabulous 561 pounds.

The next day we missed a medium-sized white marlin, but it scarcely mattered. We were ahead of the next team by close on a hundred pounds, and the contest was ours. At the presentation celebrations, I received the trophy and a collection of engraved silverware as a lasting reminder of my first ever big-game tournament. Several months later I was awarded another, surprise, trophy. Bob Ablanalp presented me with the silver-mounted bill of the 561-pound fish. That trophy, now displayed on a wall at home, is a reminder of the year I won the World Tournament and fulfilled another dream.

The winning fish. A 610 lb blue marlin taken by Arch Lowry of New Orleans in the early 1980s.

In March 1980 I was invited to defend my title—this time partnered by Bob Ablanalp's son John, a keen young angler with a lot of big-fish experience. I arrived on Walker's Cay two days before the start of the tournament to give myself plenty of time to settle in and to talk tactics with my new partner. John already had a number of good marlin and blue fin tuna to his credit; now he wanted to achieve a win or at least a place in the Walker's Cay tournament. But it was not to be our year. We got off to a reasonable start when John put a fair-sized sailfish in the boat, but then our luck ran out. For two days, while other anglers were catching well, we did not raise a fish. Then on the fourth day I boated a white marlin weighing 105 pounds. That, we thought, should at least make us certain to win the trophy for white marlin and so get us some sort of recognition. Even that consolation prize escaped us. Ten minutes after my fish had been weighed a boat came in with a 120-pound white marlin aboard.

At least we had caught fish and weighed-in, which was more than a good many contestants had managed to do. Some had been very unlucky. One boat had run over a big fish while it was being gaffed and the propeller had cut the fish badly. Several others had their catches mauled by sharks. One competitor hit a giant blue marlin that was big enough to win the tournament outright, only to have it shark-bitten in the last stages of the battle. The shark responsible was a minute blue shark and it left a bite mark no larger than an orange. Nonetheless this marlin, like all the other damaged fish, was effectively lost; it is a tournament rule that all mutilated fish are disqualified. This may sound hard but the reasoning behind the rule is that a mutilated fish is unable to fight at full strength. Several skippers argued the point in 1980, but the judges refused to bend the rules. A marine biologist was always present at the weigh-ins to sex and age the fish, a process which often entails the fish being opened up. One blue marlin, a magnificent 440-pounder, was found to contain the complete but partially digested skeleton of a white marlin measuring six feet from beak to tail. I photographed these remains while they were still with the captor marlin's body. This was irrefutable evidence that large marlin are highly effective predators, capable of hunting down and eating prey of great size. It follows that for big fish the average-sized marlin mullet or artificial lure is definitely on the small side.

I could hardly count my second expedition to Walker's Cay an unqualified

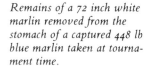

Remains of a 72 inch white marlin removed from the stomach of a captured 448 lb blue marlin taken at tournament time.

success; nevertheless, before I left the island I was invited to take part in the next year's tournament. It so happened that when I got back to England I was contacted by a television production company which wanted to make a marlin film both for the networks and for the home-video market. Since one requirement for the film was an exotic venue it seemed a good idea to combine film making with the Walker's Cay tournament. This project did not proceed with immaculate smoothness—in less than three months we lived through half a dozen changes of production company. Nonetheless, in time for the 1981 tournament, all the elements seemed to come together. There were last-minute hitches: the film crew arrived at Walker's Cay and several days later I arrived; the film's producer and director, however, did not turn up. Within a few days, though, all the stragglers had put in their appearance and we were able to start the preliminary filming. Initially it was all location work, utilizing the magnificent backdrop of the islands. By this time most of the competing boats were in the marina and excitement was running high. This was to be the largest tournament so far, with at least 85 boats taking part. The island took on a gala feeling: a local band played nightly on the docks and most owners hosted cocktail parties or noisy 'keg' parties at their berths. The clubhouse restaurant surpassed itself, serving 'reef and beef' (lobster and steak), local fish dishes and the island's celebrated conch (the locals pronounce it 'conk') and salad. This dish, which is conch flesh marinated in lime juice, has

Two competitors with a 110 lb bull dolphin. The trick with dorado (dolphin) is to locate a shoal.

Looking down on the jetties of Walker's Cay from the top of the hill.

always seemed to me the most delicious in the Bahamian repertoire.

It was also the dish most favoured by my tournament partner, who this year was rock star Roger Daltrey of 'The Who'. The television production company had wanted for their film a 'celebrity' to pull in the viewers—and who better than that keen fisherman and old friend, Roger? He flew in to the Cay on a day of uncharacteristically bad weather; rain and high winds made the approach of his plane to the runway look decidedly dangerous. Roger was unruffled; he was his usual calm self as he came off the plane. I admit that I was a little uneasy about his presence on the island—I had seen some of the mass hysteria that can greet a pop star as famous as him. My worries turned out to be totally unnecessary. Throughout his stay on the island he was treated simply as another contestant—a few autographs were requested and duly given, but mostly people addressed him by name, shook hands and moved on.

Our boat was the *Hobo* skippered by a Floridian called Jack Whittaker. We took part in the traditional tournament start, with each captain gunning his engines to race the rest of the boats to the favoured hotspot areas. The film crew shot this pulse-quickening scene from a helicopter flying overhead. We might have won the tournament on that first day. Roger rose two marlin. One hooked up instantly but made half a dozen jumps and bounced itself to freedom. The other, which was smaller, seemed unable to make up its mind—it raced up, carefully examined each bait and then turned and vanished into an indigo sea.

After this, and through the next three days, we saw no fish apart from one lone barracuda. Then, at half past three in the afternoon of the last day, Roger hooked a small tuna—too small to fight on the 80-pound class tackle we were using. As Roger brought it near the boat I saw a long, dark shadow ease up behind it—a shark, and a big one at that. I yelled to Roger to wind as fast as he could, but it was futile. I saw the shark open its mouth and cut the tuna cleanly in two. It was the end of the tuna and for us aboard *Hobo* the end of the tournament.

The winning weight that year was a magnificent aggregate of over 1,200 pounds, made up of four individual fish. Roger and I comforted ourselves with the thought that, while we might not have caught much in the way of fish, we had both enjoyed five days of hard fishing in an atmosphere of unrivalled competitive excitement.

I have never again fished from Walker's Cay, although my friendship with the owner and his family is as strong as ever. The Cay is still the Valhalla of Bahamian fishing, where good food, good fishing, and good company come together in beautiful surroundings. I have been privileged to fish there.

2
Azure Azores
A Reachable Dream

The Azores are nine lovely islands, mountains in the sea rearing up from the Mid-Atlantic Ridge—green and fertile peaks edged with great volcanic cliffs that drop down into an indigo ocean.

Owned by Portugal, the islands were first settled in the 15th century and ever since they have provided shelter for sailing ships, first for the great windships of the past and then for the smaller, swifter trans-Atlantic yachts of today. In the great days of the American whaling industry, two of the islands in particular, Fayal and Pico, supplied American whalers with crewmen and harpooners, so beginning a close relationship with America that persists to this day. Most Azoreans have relatives and friends in America, many of them still working as seamen or fishermen.

Each of the nine islands is different from its neighbours. Each retains to this day its own unique life style. But all the islands are unspoiled. There are more tourists in the islands than there used to be, but tourism has not overwhelmed the islands as it has so much of the world.

I fell in love with the islands and their people on my first visit, more than twenty years ago. I went initially to study the traditional open-boat whaling industry of the islands. Later I returned as the guest of the regional government, to explore the possibility of establishing a sport-fishing industry in the archipelago. By then I had begun to realize the sport-fishing potential of the area, although at first I thought only in terms of shark fishing—for at that time to most European fishermen sport fishing meant shark.

During these early exploratory expeditions I caught many huge mako and blue shark as well as a number of big eye tuna. Then, in 1980, I noticed the beginnings of change. Gradually, the sea-water temperature was starting to rise and with the rising temperature came new species of fish. The first new-comer I saw was a white-tip shark that appeared suddenly beside our boat and accepted a bait. It gave us a new European record for the species. In that first year a few more white tips came—big bull-headed creatures that showed little fear of our boat. They snapped up baits instantly and chased other sharks from the feeding area. Over the next two seasons this influx of white-tip shark increased as local water temperatures continued to rise annually.

At about this time I began to suspect the presence of marlin around the islands. I had little evidence to support my hunch, although as long ago as 1953

a white marlin had been taken in the vicinity of Santa Maria island. At this
stage in my discovery of the Azores I was working with a newly formed
sport-fishing company from San Miguel island. This company, Pescatur,
owned three boats and had, I thought, all the enthusiasm necessary to make a
great success out of a sport-fishing venture. Head of the company was Francisco Van Uden, now a good friend who has shared with me a great many big
fish and more than a few records. As soon as he heard me air my views about
marlin Francisco obtained a batch of artificial lures and began a trolling
campaign in the true traditions of marlin fishing. It was by then the end of the
1982 season, but despite the late start three big fish were hooked—although
only one, a fine 500 pounder, was boated. The other two remembered ap-
pointments in the West Indies and ran out line until the reel knot was reached.

Such a start made it clear that dedicated fishing could produce some interesting results. None of us realized just how interesting. The following season I
planned my trip to the Azores for early September—traditionally a good
month for mid-Atlantic weather. Something went wrong. Originally, I had
intended to fish off Fayal, but because of engine failure on one boat I found
myself marooned on San Miguel. During the first three days the weather was

perfect, but I was forced to stay on shore while a party of Scandinavian anglers was bringing in marlin weighing up to 720 pounds. Finally, my opportunity to fish came—and with it a shrieking, sea-tearing gale that lasted for more than seven days. When we did manage to get to sea, there were only two days to go before my departure date and conditions were far from perfect—the gale had left a huge swell on the ocean, making it difficult to drag big lures. Nonetheless, on the first day I had a heavy strike. I hooked up into a fish that dived deep so that I knew it to be tuna. To say I was disappointed would be an understatement. Tuna are great fighters, game creatures that probably put up a harder fight than any other fish in the sea. Unfortunately, they fight deep, diving at the first second of the hook-up to fight a slogging unseen battle hundreds of feet beneath the boat. Marlin seldom do this. Mostly they fight on the surface, in a dazzling display of raw temper that no other fish can equal. The fish I had hooked turned out to be a 70-kilo big eye tuna that fought for every inch of line I gained. It was in the boat in a fairly short time. Then I geared up for giant blue marlin and for the rest of the day we trolled over normally productive marlin water without a further strike.

28

Francisco Van Uden and Vittorio Pinho stand by the author's record blue marlin at Fayal.

With only one more day to go things looked bleak. That week of heavy storms might well have put paid to any chance of a marlin that season and we all knew it.

The next day dawned bright and clear. We left harbour at 8 o'clock in the morning, our destination the 100-fathom drop-off at the western end of the island. The sea conditions were still far from perfect, but the swells had lessened and the big bright Kona Head lures appeared to be working well. Years of fishing marlin on artificial baits had shown that a bait which moved smoothly through the water raised more fish. Short choppy seas that caused a bait to jump and dive seldom produced much action. On this day, the sea had calmed sufficiently for the baits to swim reasonably well. Despite this the morning and early afternoon passed without sign of a fish.

By this stage we were all convinced that the marlin season was effectively over. Then, at 4 o'clock, the big reel on the flat line suddenly started to sing. Almost immediately I was aware of a huge black fish breaking the surface of the water some fifty yards astern. I saw it silhouetted against the late afternoon sun and estimated its weight at somewhere between 700 and 800 pounds. It came crashing out of the water in a series of high leaps, greyhounding back across the surface to crash through the waves and finally disappear, dragging yard after yard of heavy line behind it. It was obviously well hooked-up and I thought that we now had a fighting chance of putting a big fish in the boat. There was only an hour or two to go before full dark, but if necessary I was prepared to stay until midnight.

As it happened I did not have the opportunity to fight it out. The fish must have passed over some underwater obstruction that severed the dacron line. I can still recall my sick feeling as I realized that this fish, my only marlin of that season, had gone forever. Most of all I was saddened by the knowledge that the fish still had the lure embedded in its hard bird-like mouth and was dragging several hundred yards of heavy dacron line. It would be dead within days unless it was lucky enough to shake free of the bait and I knew that, realistically, the chances of the great hook coming out of the iron mouth were very slight.

This is fishing—at one moment the total elation of being hooked to a very big, very angry and very hard-fighting fish, the next that sick feeling in the pit of the stomach when you realize that the fish that you have worked so hard and so long for has gone, and gone completely.

Naturally we carried on fishing, we fished right through the area until just after dark. Once we did raise a fish. It came up behind the lure but made no attempt to feed; it did not attack the bait, or lift its beak to rap the bait as it would normally do when feeding; it simply flashed and turned away. It was probably a fish that had seen baits before—maybe one that had been hooked and lost, maybe one that was just a little bit wiser than the others.

That was my marlin fishing for 1983. I had hooked a fish and lost it, I had seen another fish and I had missed many good days of fishing because of bad weather.

I returned to the Azores in the following August, intending to stay for three weeks and, given reasonable luck, to fish for marlin every day. As soon as I landed, at the port of Horta on Fayal, I discovered that during the week of my

It is the clarity of the water in the Seven Cities Lake that gives the fishing an extra edge.

The author with his Hardy shoulder harness, having landed a 660 lb marlin.

Snap photograph by the author of a dolphin jumping as it passes an Azorean whale boat.

arrival marlin fishing had been hectic. A visiting angler had boated six fish and raised many more. During seven days' fishing he had been broken many times and sometimes totally spooled—that is, he had lost every inch of line to a running fish. Clearly he had encountered some very large marlin indeed. To make matters even more interesting he had raised and hooked-up a number of white marlin, any one of which would have qualified as a new European record. Oddly enough, though, his best catch had been surprisingly small—a mere 400-pounder.

To call a fish of 400 pounds 'surprisingly small' would be ridiculous in most of the world's blue marlin centres. The Azores area is, however, unique; it has huge marlin in super abundance. Nobody is sure where they originate. One school of thought holds that they come from the African coast, but my own feeling is that they come from beyond the West Indies. If this is so they must pass a long way outside the island groups in a mid-ocean migration that finally brings them to the mid-Atlantic islands of the Azores. One clue to their origin may lay in the parasitical remora fish that they bring with them. Practically every large Azorean blue marlin is host to strange blue-white remora fish that are unlike any other remora I have seen. Hopefully, these fish will help us trace the marlin's migration route.

I arrived on a Friday afternoon, and spent the remainder of the day checking tackle and rigging lures, traces and hooks—in general making full preparations for an early start the next morning. For the first week of my stay I was

to fish with a Pescatur captain, Luis Lajes. Originally from mainland Portugal,
Luis had spent many years in the Portuguese navy. Then he had married a girl
from San Miguel and left the navy. For several seasons he had skippered the
Pescatur boat *Rabao*. Small but tough, with an outrageous sense of humour, he
had a great ability to find fish. Nothing frightened him and he was altogether
a good man to fish with.

  He was also a good friend of mine and so, with the boat and tackle shipshape, it was only natural that we should celebrate. Fayal is an ideal place for
celebrations of this sort—the local people are friendly and receptive, everyone
seems to be out to have a good time and the bars stay open late. One of these
bars is the Café Sport in Horta, run by my old friend Peter Azevedho, which is
one of the most famous yachting bars in the world. Transatlantic yachts from
all over the world use Horta harbour as a stopover base and their crews
gravitate naturally towards Peter's for mail, food, coffee and of course alcoho-
lic beverage—his gin-and-tonics are famous with yachtsmen everywhere.

  So it was at Peter's that Luis and I renewed our friendship. Food and drink
are very cheap in the Azores, so a happy evening costs very little. From the
Café Sport we wandered up through the main harbour area to the Club
Naval—another bar well known to sailors from all other the world. This year

the Club Naval had a new owner, Vittorio Pinho. Vittorio was a Portuguese who had spent much of his life abroad but had now returned to the Azores and taken over the Club Naval with the intention of turning it into a first-class restaurant. He and I quickly became fast friends and throughout my stay on the island Vittorio made sure that when we came in after a day's fishing, even very late at night, we could get a good meal to set us up for an early start the following morning. By the time we reached the Club Naval Luis and I had met many people we had known in previous years or on other islands and my first evening had turned as it always does into a party. Red wine flowed freely and someone produced a bottle of the old Pico wine. I don't know what time we left the Club Naval, but my head had hardly touched the pillow when it was time to wake up and get ready for sea. The day dawned bright and beautiful and across from Horta harbour I could see the great volcanic peak of Pico island shining in the brilliant morning sunlight.

As we headed out through the harbour entrance and the first lures splashed gaudily into the water, some instinct told me that on this day I was going to catch my first Azorean marlin. We had gone no more than 300 yards past the point of the island when I had a strike on one lure. The fish was there for only a second before it was gone, but I was sure it wasn't a marlin. Two hundred yards further on we had a second strike, but this time the fish was on. Obviously, though, it was not a big fish. As I wound it up to the back of the boat Luis made ready with the gaff and seconds later in came the first wahoo ever caught in the Azores. I had caught many big wahoo in the West Indies and I was delighted to find that they were now in the Azores area—yet more proof that the waters were warming up. My specimen weighed just 16 kilos and was subsequently entered as a new European record. Later that night, back at the Club Naval, Vittorio grilled it on his open fire; it made a delicious meal.

Less than five minutes later I hooked a huge blue marlin. As the fish jumped repeatedly and took many hundreds of yards of line we could all see that it was a very large fish, probably in excess of 700 pounds. Unfortunately, after many splendid jumps and five minutes of concentrated fighting, we saw it leap in the air and throw the lure clear of its iron jaw. Disappointed but not defeated we carried on and had covered less than another 100 yards when a second fin came up astern of a bright red-and-gold Kona Head lure, and we watched as the beak raised to club the bait into submission. This one hooked-up solidly and fought extremely well. Later, on shore, it weighed in at 160 kilos. This was my first blue marlin from the Azores and a fish that I was justifiably proud of. Interestingly enough, when hooked the fish made no attempt to jump; instead it dived, taking many hundreds of yards of line with it. Once down into deep water it fought a hard, slogging battle, reminiscent of the fight of a shark. Later, I discovered that many Azorean blue marlin fight in this way. The smaller fish tend to dive when hooked; larger fish put up a much more spectacular surface battle in traditional blue-marlin style.

It was still early in the day and with one blue marlin already in the boat I had hopes of further sport. We continued to troll the same area; on our left lay the island of Pico with San Jorge behind it and before us was the blue island of Fayal. The whole scene was set for big fish and it wasn't long before another fish came up and took a lure. This time it was a white marlin. White marlin seem to lead charmed lives and this one was no exception. It came up hard and fast, wrapped the bait solidly with its bill, turned and took the lure into its mouth, apparently hooking itself in the process. After a magnificent first run and a number of high jumps, it turned again, ran back towards the boat and passed us at high speed, leaping from the water every few yards. This fish was like all white marlin—what it lacked in size it made up for in confidence and courage. It jumped and jumped as though it were a giant blue marlin and finally the inevitable happened and the lure flew out of its beak. Disappointing as this was, none of us in the boat was worried; we had already seen plenty of marlin and we were confident of another strike before many more minutes had passed. Sure enough, with the engines holding the boat at a steady 8 knots, we had travelled only 400 or 500 yards before yet another marlin came up, took the bait and hooked itself. Instantly it became airborne, putting on the dramatic show of aerobatics that only a light-weight billfish can produce. Several times it jumped totally clear of the water and I could see the lure

European record white marlin for the author.

hanging from the corner of its bird-like beak. But white marlin are notorious for jumping off and that is what this fish did. I was still not discouraged. I knew that we were in an area thick with marlin, both white and blue, and I was sure that we would hook-up again on yet another big fish. But then the sea went strangely quiet; there were no birds around us and the schools of dolphin had deserted us. We rode a placid sea in a silence broken only by the sound of the boat's engines. This interlude lasted for perhaps two hours and we were just beginning to feel that the marlin shoals had passed us by, when I distinctly heard a snap of the outrigger pin and the scream of the reel. I turned to see a huge fish tail-walking across the surface of the water. It was a blue marlin, and a very big fish indeed. The water was whipped to foam as the marlin tore out line. It seemed to be well hooked and I felt that given time we could bring it to the boat. I had it for nearly one hour, but as it came closer to the boat and just as we saw it clearly for the first time, the hook simply dropped free of its jaw. It was a bitter disappointment. The fish was big—my estimation was over 700 pounds and it could have topped 800 pounds.

Francisco Van Uden heaving in a medium marlin: note the very necessary tough leather gloves!

Fighting a big blue marlin taken on a yellow-and-green lure. Most rod-caught marlin are taken on natural or artificial baits, trolled at surface level.

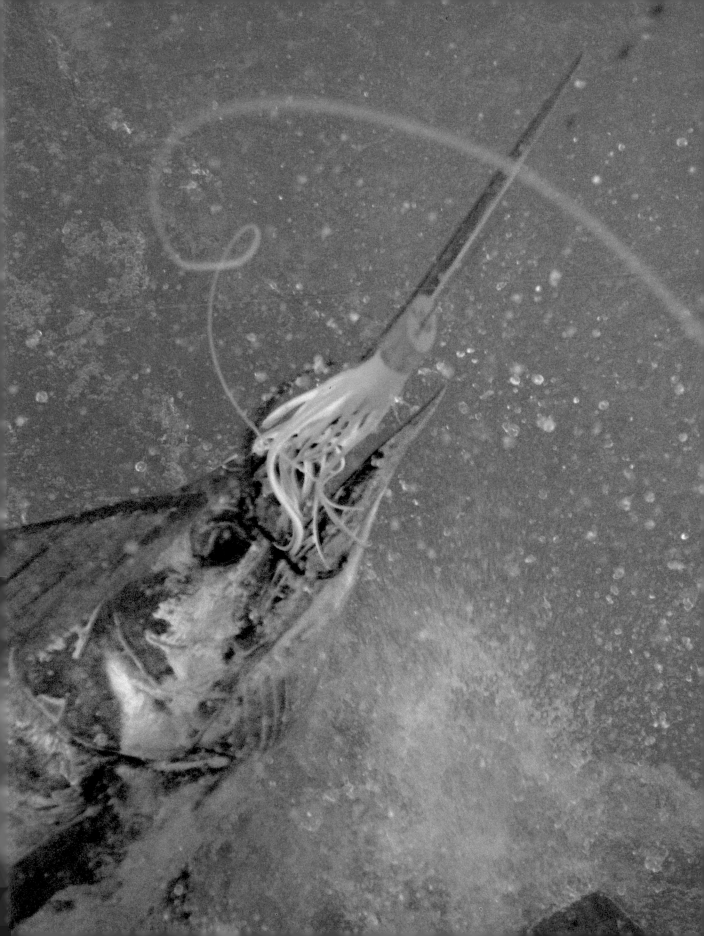

Francisco Van Uden with 570 lb blue marlin.

Soon after, we turned back for Horta; as we entered harbour the sun was just sinking away to the westward beyond the black mountain. With the fish weighed and in the cold store, we headed for the Café Sport and a much-needed gin-and-tonic. Later, at the Club Naval with a good meal inside us, we looked back on the day's fishing. We had lost a number of fish, but we didn't fault ourselves for this; we had just had a typical run of marlin fishing bad luck—when lure fishing for marlin you can expect a good 85 per cent of all fish hooked to come off before they can be boated. There is little the angler can do about this; the hooks can be set only after the fish has struck, at the instant when the boat is moving forward and the fish has taken the lure and is going away in the opposite direction.

I promised myself an early night, but as usual on Fayal I met a number of old friends and we sat and talked into the early hours of the morning. Despite my lack of sleep I was up at dawn, looking out across the harbour to see the sun come up between San Jorge and Pico—one of the most splendid sights in the world. I got down to the boat to find that skipper Luis was ready to sail. We headed for the same area as before, at the point of the island—we had found so many fish there yesterday that it was unthinkable to fish anywhere else. Soon after clearing the point I had a solid strike from a white marlin—a nice little fish, well hooked, that stayed on the line and fought a hard, long battle against heavy tackle. Little fish like this are capable, despite their lack of weight, of putting up a remarkable battle even on the strongest of tackle. This time the hook held firm and it was not too long before we were able to gaff the fish and drag it aboard. It weighed only 32 kilos, but it constituted a new European record. Skipper Luis was so delighted that he picked up the fish and kissed it.

We had the taste for marlin now and could hardly wait to get the next. We trolled for another 30 minutes, seeing very little, then a huge blue marlin came up behind one of the baits. It was probably the biggest blue marlin that I have ever seen in my life—between 16 and 18 feet long and weighing something approaching 2,000 pounds. Aboard the boat we could scarcely believe what we were seeing. But the great fish just looked at the bait and turned away. We never saw it again. Soon afterwards another white marlin came to investigate us; it took a red-and-yellow Kona Head, hooked itself solidly on the take and began to dance across the waves. A great blue marlin breaking the surface is a really spectacular sight, but a white marlin is far more fascinating to watch. It leaves the water more clearly and evenly than does its heavier blue cousin, showing its full length above the water, and its jumps are higher, longer and more graceful. This one was no exception, but ten minutes later it was in the boat and I had the second white marlin of the trip—and a fish that again broke the white marlin record.

The most effective artificial lure yet developed for marlin —the Kona Head. The lures should be fished in the wake of your boat.

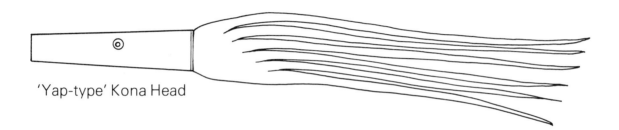

'Yap-type' Kona Head

We had thoughts then of the hat-trick—three white marlin in one day— but it was not to be. We had two more strikes from white marlin, both of which apparently hooked themselves, but then bounced off leaving us to wind in the slack line. Later we had a strike from a very big blue marlin which ran 300 or 400 yards, jumping all the way, before finally throwing all the hooks high and clear of its beak. Cursing my luck, I reflected again on the charmed lives that marlin seem to enjoy.

Nonetheless, we had had a good day's fishing by anybody's standards. We had twice broken a white marlin record, hooked two more white marlin and lost a very big blue marlin. All the signs were that it was only a matter of time before we found a concentration of huge fish.

Knucklehead lures are extremely effective for white marlin. Once attracted to a bait white marlin tend to be less prone to alarm than blue marlin.

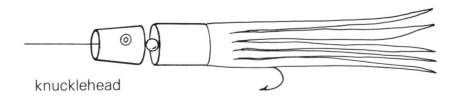

knucklehead

Next day we were joined by Vittorio, who had done some fishing in Africa and was keen to experience game fishing in his own home waters. Again, the weather was near perfect, a flat, calm sea with only the slightest suggestion of a swell—perfect trolling weather. As we headed once more for the point of the island we could see thousands of birds wheeling and diving about a mile offshore. Such activity meant that either marlin or dolphin were driving bait fish to the surface. On arrival we could see that much of the activity was created by a huge pack of common dolphin. Passing through the dolphin pack it was fascinating to watch these lovely creatures jump and swim behind and in front of us. Several had young with them, diminutive little rascals that raced alongside their mothers to ride and play in our bow wave. The amazing thing about dolphin is that they never make a pass at an artificial bait. In many years spent trolling all over the world, I have never seen or heard of a dolphin taking an angler's bait. Such is the intelligence of these graceful animals that they can discern instantly that a bait or lure has hooks buried beneath its gaudy body. If marlin had the intelligence to see this no one would ever have the chance to catch them; fortunately, marlin are not so clever. And, given the abundance of fish life that now surrounded us, hopefully marlin would not be far away. As we left the dolphins behind us I climbed to the bridge to watch for marlin birds—delicate shearwaters that seem to mark and follow their chosen fish like submarine-tracking helicopters. Wherever these little brown-headed seabirds are, there too will be feeding marlin. I soon spotted a line of them not far away across the water and Luis turned the boat to follow them. At that moment I heard a heavy splash followed instantly by the scream of a tortured reel.

Vittorio was nearest to the rod and I shouted to him to take the fish. For a man who had done little big-game fishing he reacted well. Instantly, he swept the big rod out of its holder and threw himself into the fighting chair. Moments later a huge blue marlin surfaced and began to speed away across the water. Luis and I looked at each other in despair; the fish was a monster, weighing at the very least 300 kilos, and the man in the chair had no experience of handling such a fish. To be frank we fully expected the marlin to break free. But we had under-rated Vittorio. Perhaps he had never before caught a marlin, but he had read and digested every game-fishing book that had come his way. Perhaps he was a trout angler by instinct, but he had caught tiger fish in the Zambezi and shark off Maputo Island. He had the mind and, as we were soon to see, the heart of a great angler. Soon after hooking the fish he asked us what we thought it weighed. Not wanting to alarm him, we lied. Maybe 200 kilos, certainly no more, we told him. 'Big enough for a beginner,' he replied happily.

After half an hour of savage action the fish was still jumping. Vittorio was beginning to suffer the pain that all big-game anglers know—from straining back and protesting arm muscles. The smile had gone from his face and he had no energy to spare for banter now. He was learning the whole truth of marlin fishing; it was just he alone against the fish. From the dogged look on his face I knew that he was determined to bring the fish home; he still believed the fish to be in the medium weight range and we made no attempt to disillusion him. During the next 50 minutes he fought a hard, bitter battle for every inch of line gained. Finally the fish was in sight, a huge electric blue shadow that lay

The author's record 855 lb blue marlin taken aboard the Rabao. *The Azores, being mid-Atlantic islands, are ideally placed for taking the great Atlantic big-game species.*

388 Kg
AZORES
15.9.85
PESCATUR

AZORES
15.9.85

BIG GAME
FISHING AZORES
DATE 15·9·85
ANGLER TREVOR
HOUSBY
FISH BLUE MARLIN
WEIGHT 388 Kg
BOAT - "RABÃO"
PESCATUR

off the stern of the boat. At this stage neither the fish nor Vittorio gained or lost much line—if the fish managed to take a yard or two, Vittorio cranked it back to its original position. Game-fishing stalemate! The trick at such times is always to keep the line tight. Fortunately Vittorio had realized that after so protracted a struggle the hook could be on the verge of tearing out and that an inch of slack line could easily lose the marlin forever. He worked his fish like a professional, never once relaxing the rod pressure. Time and again the double line almost reached the rod tip before the fish, sensing danger, slowly moved away from the boat. Finally, however, Vittorio's grim determination to succeed overcame the vast brute strength of the fish. First the knot on the double line inched back through the rings to bury itself on the big reel. Slowly but surely the trace swivel rose from the water to snick up against the tip ring of the big rod. At this point I whispered to Vittorio to slacken the reel drag slightly, just in case the fish made one last desperate bid for freedom. At the same instant the mate and skipper Luis went into action. The mate grasped the heavy nylon leader to pull the fish to the boat and Luis leaned over to set the first big gaff solidly. For the next few moments all of us were too active to take notice of Vittorio. Only when the fish had been 'tail' roped and fully secured did the handshakes and back slaps begin. The fish was huge, so big that we were unable to heave it into the boat and had instead to tie it alongside. Luis sat on its head to make it fast to the boat's cleats; with his legs dangling into the dark blue water he looked like the 'Boy on a Dolphin'. Vittorio could hardly believe what had happened—time and again he leaned over the side to admire his catch.

Later, on Fayal, the fish was weighed in at 350 kilos—a true ocean giant and a hard fish to conquer. That night at Vittorio's restaurant we dined on grilled blue-marlin steaks washed down with an endless supply of superb red wine that I suspect Vittorio had been keeping for just such an occasion.

The next day I brought in two marlin, a white of 34 kilos and a blue of 220 kilos. But again I was plagued by bad luck—twice I hooked up on huge fish only to have them run out a lot of line and jump themselves off the hooks. Then the weather changed; bright sunshine gave way to storm clouds that brought a savage wind in their wake. From my hotel room I could look down on the harbour, and as I saw it begin to fill with huge ocean-going tuna catchers I knew we were in for many days of bad weather. To lose fishing time when there were so many marlin in the area was a tragedy, and as the days of inactivity slid by I became more and more despondent.

During this period Luis went back to San Miguel to see his family and my good friend Francisco Van Uden flew out to take his place, bringing with him two South African anglers, Piet Jacobs and Piet Bingles. The bad weather frustrated their plans too, but finally, on the last day of the South Africans' stay, our luck changed. The wind died down overnight and by morning the weather was kind enough for us to get in some fishing. It was left to me to decide on the fishing ground and, although I was tempted to return to the point of the island, I decided to fish instead in the area of the Condor Bank. The Condor is in fact the peak of an underwater mountain reaching to within 100 fathoms of the surface; its sides fall away into a mighty submerged canyon, many thousands of feet deep. Its waters are rich in fish life and this

Author with a medium blue marlin taken the day before the record was broken.

BIG GAME
FISHING AZORES
DATE 14·9·85
ANGLER TREVOR
HOUSBY
FISH BLUE MARLIN
WEIGHT 285 Kg
BOAT - "RABÃO"

readily available food supply attracts giant predators to the area. Over the years the Condor has given me many big fish—white tips, blues and mighty mako shark. Now I thought it would also produce marlin.

As we ran up the coast past the majestic rock called Castello Branco and out over the lovely Varradouro Bay we made ready our tackle—checking knots, sharpening hooks and examining traces for the tiny nicks that could so easily cause them to part under fighting pressure. When everything was shipshape we ran out the lures while Francisco throttled back the boat to trolling speed. The South Africans, who during their enforced idleness on Fayal had heard every marlin story in the Azores' repertoire, were eager for action. Piet Jacobs in particular was fishing with a purpose. He had fished black marlin in Australia, but had come to the opinion that Australian fishing was now only a pale shadow of its former glory; he found the Australian season too short and the price of fishing too high. Consequently, he thought that he might divert many South African anglers from Australia to the Azores, but he was sceptical of the stories he had heard and wanted to find out for himself whether Azores fishing was as exciting as he had been invited to believe. Knowing this, Francisco, with a sharp eye to business, was keen to show him some sport.

We were less than three miles from the Condor when a big fish hit one of our lures—it was, I remember, a strange blue lure of South African design. I had agreed that the visitors should take the first two strikes, and as Jacobs was nearest the rod it was he who threw himself into the fighting chair and braced himself to do battle. But after a short run the fish jumped itself off and escaped. Jacobs, a lawyer by profession, used language that would have had him barred from any court in the world. Who could blame him? He had flown thousands of miles and sat through days of Atlantic gales only to lose, on his final day, an impressively big blue marlin.

It was only then that I appreciated how little credence he had given to our stories. 'That's it,' he said despondently, 'the only chance of the day gone!' The idea that Azorean marlin tend to shoal was totally unbelievable to him. But I had spotted a few wheeling shearwater and I told him and an almost equally incredulous Piet Bingles to stand by the rods. We had travelled no more than 100 yards before the line snapped clear of the outrigger as a huge fish hit a gaudy green-and-yellow lure. The second it felt the hook it became airborne in big-marlin style, rising almost in slow motion, its huge beak wagging while its vast tail sent fountains of white water skyward. Piet Bingles took one look at the fish and settled in for a grim session in the chair. He was a big man, but he knew he would need every ounce of his strength in the fight ahead. The marlin was magnificent, a great open-ocean predator feeling fear for the first time in its life. Like so many big marlin it seemed to blame its misfortune on the bait that hung from its jaw. We lost count of the number of times it leapt—hardly had the water settled behind it than once again it was up and away across the waves. With an hour gone Piet was beginning to tire. You can be the strongest man in the world, but it takes more than strength alone to fight a big-game fish. Eighty minutes into the struggle and Piet was no longer aware of our presence. His world was empty of everything except himself and the fish. I knew what was going through his mind—the love, hate, fear and mental exhaustion of fighting a fish of this calibre can play strange tricks on an angler.

Piet Jacobs chose this moment to inform us that this was his partner's first ever billfish. This was a baptism of fire. Strangely, I was sure that Piet would boat this one; the goddess of fortune was with us, giving my guests the chance of a monster as their first fish. Fortunately I have never been 'fish jealous' and, although I would have given my soul to be tied to Piet's giant, I never doubted that my love of the beautiful islands of the Azores would, sooner or later, be rewarded with a marlin of my own that would make the world sit up and take notice. Finally Piet's fish was ready for gaffing. It came easily at the end—a great, defeated creature that still looked every inch an ocean warrior. With the gaffs in, it was simply a matter of controlled hard work to drag its great body into the cockpit of the boat. It was what the Americans would call a 'moose', a monster—larger even than Vittorio's 350-kilo fish.

We celebrated with a quick beer and 20 minutes later I was in the chair slogging it out with a fish of unknown size that made no attempt to jump at any stage of the 30-minute battle. I knew from the onset that this was a flyweight in comparison to Piet Bingles' fish. Later, it weighed in at 120 kilos. Piet's fish weighed 360 kilos—a big blue marlin by anyone's standards.

After I had boated my fish Piet Jacobs hooked up his second strike of the day and fought a good 200-kilo fish to a standstill in exactly an hour. But sadly, as the mate grasped the leader, the lure dropped out and with a weary flick of its lovely tail the marlin went back to its blue, cold world. Even then the activity was not over. In less than an hour we hooked and lost three more fish—each jumped off after the usual dazzling display of aerobatics. Finally, with full dark only minutes away, we called it a day.

Back in Horta, Piet Bingles took us all out to dinner in celebration of his fish. The red wine of Pico flowed like water to fire the blood and lubricate the mind. It was another long, late session during which the talk was all fishing. When the South Africans left the next morning they swore to be back: their short stay had been enough to show them the special magic of the Azores.

I still had four days left and I was determined to make the most of my time. The fish, though, had other ideas. The weather was perfect but the marlin had vanished. Francisco was in despair. I, now with just two days to go, was still determined to fish hard and long in a final attempt to catch a giant blue marlin. I was convinced that the fish were out there—the question was, where? Weighing up all the possibilities, I decided to stick it out in the Condor Bank area. Instinct told me that the marlin were still there, hunting and feeding in deep water close to the top of the bank.

The Condor is a fishing ground out of a dream; it has a magical quality. To me it is a very special place. I never fish there without experiencing a sharp, trembling feeling of anticipation—for there, I am sure, leviathan fish wait to be hooked. I have lost track of the many battles I have fought on the Bank— some successful, some depressingly unsuccessful. Some things that have happened to me there have been totally unexplainable. Like the day I fished a large live bait deep down, in the hope of a big shark. I had never before fished a bait at this depth and was surprised to feel a strong pull as the bait swam down. The bait was taken with confidence and hooking-up was a formality. That was when I realized that I had hooked something of unusual strength and size. The fish set off immediately to the north-east; there was no rush, no panic, just a steady strong run that pulled yard after yard of heavy line off the 120 reel. I maintained constant heavy rod pressure, which seemed to make no impression at all on the running fish. Suddenly, with over 200 yards of line out, the fish was gone. When I wound in I found that the big swivel that joined the trace to the double line had been bitten cleanly in half through the barrel section. The fish, I am sure, was a shark (although it didn't indulge in a shark's typical head-shaking routine). But what kind of shark? I have no idea. I could only write off the incident as just another mystery of the Condor.

Conditions were near perfect as we left Horta harbour; there was scarcely a breath of wind and the blue, pellucid waters lifted serene and unruffled beneath our keel. Five miles from the bank we ran out the big lures, settled the rods in place and clipped lines into outrigger pins. I had decided to fish only three rods, all heavy—two 80-pound class rigs and one 130-pound class outfit. The light rods stayed in the cabin, this was an all or nothing day. I had chosen the lures carefully. On the right rigger was a dark blue South African lure with a drilled-out head and additional jet holes angled to send off streams of water to add vibration to visual attraction. The left rigger carried a green-and-yellow lure and the flat line a red-and-yellow jointed lure. All were known to be highly attractive to marlin. We passed over the area where Piet Bingles had

Vittorio Pinho and the author, with Pinho's first ever marlin, weighing in at 770 lb.

boated his big fish without sighting a marlin. Then, just as Francisco signalled that we had reached the top of the Bank, a 500-pound-plus marlin shot into sight, rapped the blue bait with its bill and snatched the line out of the outrigger pin. At exactly the same instant a second marlin took the lure from the flat line. With two fish on at once I had to make an instant decision. I took the first marlin, dropping quickly into the fighting chair as the hooked fish began its dancing run towards the horizon. The mate cranked the reel handle on the second rod, but we were really hoping that the second fish would jump itself off. None of us could have anticipated what happened next. My fish was displaying on the surface over 300 yards away and the second fish was in the air 40 yards off the boat, when to my horror I saw that my line was actually in the mouth of the mate's fish. It must have swum straight into the taut line and somehow managed to get it jammed across its jaws. I knew then that I had no chance of boating my fish. The two fish were pulling against each other with a combined weight of over 800 pounds. I expected both lines to break and resigned myself to losing two expensive baits, but I was lucky—both fish threw the lures and vanished from sight leaving only a slight tangle of line to sort out. Our disappointment was intense, but at least we knew now that marlin were in the area. And confirmation of that came only seconds after we had got our baits back into the water. The South African lure brought us a big fish and this time there were no disasters. The marlin fought a hard, long surface battle that lasted just an hour. It looked to weigh close on 300 kilos, but it lost a lot of blood during gaffing and later weighed in at 285 kilos. I felt better after this success—back on form, with a big fish under my belt and another full day's fishing still to come.

We were back on the Condor very early next morning. Lines of marlin birds were already patrolling the surface. It was an encouraging sign, because if no fish are around these birds circle high in the air; when they fly a straight course low over the water it means that they are tracking marlin. We had not long to wait. Again, it was the South African lure that brought up the first fish—a medium-weight marlin that put on a ten-minute show of temper before ejecting the lure. Minutes later I was hooked into a second marlin on the same lure. At the same instant one of the other lures was struck by a smallish mako shark, which was brought rapidly to the boat and released, leaving me free to slog it out with my marlin. Mostly this fish stayed deep—only in the initial stages of the fight did it break surface, and then only briefly. Thirty-five minutes later the fish was in the boat; it was a nicely shaped little marlin that we estimated at 120 kilos. We took time out to photograph it while it was fresh, but were soon back fishing. For twenty minutes or so we saw no sign of a fish. Then a huge marlin tore down upon the blue lure and wrapped the bait with its sword-like bill. Again and again it attacked. I have no idea how many times it smashed down on the fast-moving bait, but I have certainly never seen a marlin react so frenziedly to a lure—although, oddly, it made no attempt actually to eat the bait. It sheared away in the end, but not before it had jangled my nerves beyond reason—so sure was I that the fish would take that I had had the rod ready in my hand.

Francisco spun the wheel to turn the boat and we trolled again over the same area, watching and waiting for the fish to come up again. Abruptly it was there, right up behind the bait, neon-blue lights rippling all over its body. It shot forward and nailed the bait solidly. I knew at once that this was the biggest blue marlin I had ever hooked, and strangely I also knew that I would kill it. This was a meeting that seemed predestined, and as I settled back into the fighting chair and clipped the shoulder harness on to the reel lugs, I felt good. The fish had taken on an 80-class outfit, a rig that I favoured for its flexibility—a heavier rod may kill a big fish more quickly but on the 80-pound stick I felt able to apply maximum pressure without tearing myself apart in the process. This fish was a colossus and it fought me with a power and savagery that I shall never forget. Its first mad surface rush stripped over 500 yards of line from the reel. Largely because of Francisco's skill at the wheel we rapidly regained much of this lost line. Then, 100 yards off our stern, the water erupted for the second time and the huge fish beat the water to foam as again it reared clear of the surface. In the bright afternoon sunlight the great body looked black and silver rather than blue and white; it was an awesome sight, with its flaring gills and surging beak and its long, heavy dorsal fin standing out along the ridge of its mighty back. This fish had no fear; its primitive mind could not conceive of defeat, for its strength and ability had never failed it before. It cared nothing for the boat or its occupants, instead it centred its seething anger on the bait dangling from its jaw. Twice it took line in excess of 300 yards, but each time it rose again to shake at the lure, giving me the opportunity to get most of the line back on the reel. Once it dived deep and began to tow us slowly backwards. When this did not work it rose again and again to send a spray of white water flying from the surface.

At this stage I was still having fun, but I knew that the hard work would really begin when I started to pump the fish solidly back to the boat. With an

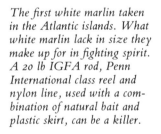

The first white marlin taken in the Atlantic islands. What white marlin lack in size they make up for in fighting spirit. A 20 lb IGFA rod, Penn International class reel and nylon line, used with a combination of natural bait and plastic skirt, can be a killer.

hour gone I could sense that the fish was wearing down and I began to pile on pressure. Now there was no time to joke with the mate, just the hard routine of raising the fish bit by bit and winding down to gain not feet but inches of line. Twice the fish pulled me to a standing position on the foot rest of the fighting chair; many times I lost yards of hard-won line. Each time, however, my back, shoulder and arm muscles worked in unison to get the lost line back. By now I was able to use my fingers on the side of the reel spool, a method of applying extra drag that can cut minutes off a long battle.

The sweat dripped from me and my back felt as though it would break at any second. The fish was just in sight, a blue shadow deep down astern of the boat. Now I was fighting for the first sign of the double line and the satisfying click of the trace swivel snicking against the top ring. Many times the double line was back on the reel only to be lost again as the tired fish forged slowly ahead. Finally, the trace swivel emerged inch by inch from the sea, drops of water falling from it as it rose, and I knew the battle was over. An hour and thirty-five minutes from hook-up we had the fish tied to the boat. For another hour we struggled to heave it inboard, but even with a rigged block and tackle the three of us could not manage to bring it more than half out of the water. Finally we tied it alongside and steamed off back to Horta, arriving at half past ten at night. We had to use a crane to lift the fish into the boat and at that time of night it was impossible to weigh it. That meant that I would never see my fish weighed, or be photographed with it. I had to be at the airport by 7 o'clock next morning.

In the morning, very early, I went down to the boat to photograph my two fish—the first one I had caught looking like a tiddler beside the second. Two days later, back in England, I learned that my colossus had weighed in at 856 pounds; it was a new European record and possibly an 80-pound class record as well.

I shall never forget the quietness as that marlin finally came to the boat, its neon-blue colour lighting up the water for yards around. The Azores had again been kind to me.

My dreams still centre on those lovely Atlantic islands. I hope to return to them many times to meet old friends again, to drink the heady local wine again and to fish again the endless azure sea.

3
Barracuda
The World's Wild Hunt

I have been fascinated by barracuda ever since my childhood, when I first read of their resemblance to the pike I knew from the streams of my own country and of their extreme ferocity. I longed then for the chance to pit my skill and strength against them.

In those youthful days of dreaming I pictured the barracuda only as a fish of the coral reefs—a long, sleek silver predator inhabiting a fantasy world of coral and surrounded by myriads of the brightly coloured reef fish that were its prey. This image, I know now, is only part of the truth. Big barracuda can be found in the vicinity of shallow reefs. Equally, however, they can be found in salt-water rivers bordered by flat green mangrove swamps, in shallow-water flats and in the open ocean many miles from the shore. They exist in various forms and great numbers from Australia to Mexico and around the islands of Madeira and the Azores.

My first experience of barracuda was at Walker's Cay in the Bahamas. From the island beaches I caught fish up to 10 or 12 pounds in weight. My technique was simple: I simply tipped the hooks of an artificial lure with a fish strip, cast out and virtually instantly made contact with a good fish. These Walker's Cay barracuda were as hungry as they were plentiful; almost every cast would produce a take. It mattered little if a fish took but was not hooked. The barracuda showed no fear and often a fish that had escaped would take again on the next cast. On light spin-fishing tackle these comparatively small barracuda fought like tigers and gave good sport. Years later I fished the same grounds in company with rock star Roger Daltrey. Roger, an experienced angler, promptly caught barracuda fever to such an extent that it was difficult to drag him away from the beaches. He told me that, as a child fishing London's Regent Canal, he had read of barracuda and had vowed that one day he would test for himself their fighting ability.

Having cut my eye teeth on the beach residents, it was a natural progression to try for bigger fish from a boat and it was at this stage that I began to learn more about barracuda. The best way to catch them was to troll with Japanese feathers, which could be made even more attractive by the addition of a fillet of ballao or ladyfish. A feather of almost any colour would catch fish, but yellow was best of all. When my Bahamian guide first told me of this colour preference I was sceptical, but I quickly realized that he was right. I used to

troll with two 20-pound class outfits and to begin with I fished yellow feathers on one rod and red-and-white on the other. But nine out of ten strikes came on the yellow feathers and I soon abandoned the red-and-white lure and used only yellow.

My catches increased dramatically and my guide became more enthusiastic when he was able to go home with a plentiful supply of big fish. The local people ate coral-reef barracuda as a staple part of their diet, although it was ill-advisable for visiting anglers to eat them. The fish were full of a poison to which the locals seemed immune, but which in others caused loss of hair, paralysis and sometimes even death. It was a classic food-chain prison starting with the small reef fish which fed on coral polyps: the small fish fed off the

European record barracuda, on a yellow lure, taken off Formigas Rocks, 70 miles from San Miguel. The European barracuda is on average far smaller than its tropical counterpart.

Gaffing a nice barracuda off Florida, U.S.A.

54

coral, the barracuda fed off the small fish and humans fed off the barracuda.

The poisonous flesh of the local barracuda was of little interest to me. My interest in the species was for the sport they gave rather than their food value. Trolling the reef areas produced enough good-sized barracuda, weighing between 20 and 30 pounds, to keep me happy—for a time.

My education in the ways of barracuda, begun on the beaches of Walker's Cay, continued. I soon discovered that the very big barracuda tended to stay offshore, sometimes as open-ocean surface feeders, more often as bottom feeders in very deep water. Then, while live-baiting for grouper, I hooked a number of very big barracuda and I also saw some monsters taken by anglers trolling for blue marlin. It was clear that natural live or dead baits were always more tempting to barracuda than artificial lures.

I was able to put this first-hand knowledge to practical use when I later fished various areas of central America. I remember one occasion in particular. I was fishing a totally unpopulated section of the coastline of Belize. The day was hot, the sky blue, the sands on the shore white and the water like glass.

Fighting a good barracuda off Walker's Cay, Bahamas.

A barracuda taken off Belize in Central America. These fish are found in tropical seas from Australia to Africa and America.

Although the area was one where big barracuda are as common as trout in a hatching pond, the sea seemed empty of fish—the barracuda's coloration camouflaged them so effectively that I only sighted a fish when one took a bait. Yet in these conditions I saw the largest barracuda that I ever expect to see. My local companion had hooked a barracuda of perhaps 20 pounds on light tackle. Suddenly, we became aware of something like a section of telegraph pole drifting towards us. At first it did not occur to us that it was a fish, but as we watched it became a gigantic barracuda that simply swam up, bit clean through the hooked fish and took away the tail half. I guessed that the

57

marauder must have weighed around 100 pounds; my companion (an excitable South American) judged it to be at least half as much again. He may have been right. It was a monster; certainly the largest barracuda I have ever seen. Even its colour was exceptional; it lacked the silver sheen of a normal barracuda and was black in the water.

Fishing on this wild coast was fun; the boats were small and the fish big. I stayed for several weeks in an Indian village whose people lived in such poverty that I have no words to describe it. The nearest town of consequence was over a hundred miles away and few of the villagers had ever been there; local nomadic trade people brought in the few products the village needed to buy from outside. Once a year the villagers set fire to the forest and shot the fleeing animals as they ran along the fire-free beaches. The resulting chaos filled me with sadness, but the Indians had no such sentiment—when an area was hunted out they simply moved on. They ate anything edible that they could lay their hands on—parrots, snakes, even monkeys. Fishing to them was important, but their equipment and techniques were far from perfect. My fine lines and rods filled them with wonder, as did my selection of baits and

A fine 80 lb barracuda in the Bahamas for a father and son fishing team from Chicago.

Boating a barracuda; note the teeth!

hooks—all of which vanished before my departure. It wasn't thieving, it was simply the only way to obtain equipment that would ensure a continuing supply of edible fish. Certainly all the barracuda I caught, and there were hundreds of them, found their way into the bellies of the local people. In such poverty all was grist to the mill.

In Belize my tally of big barracuda was enormous, but only once did I sight a fish that looked like a record-breaker—that was the 'telegraph pole' that stole half our catch. When I did eventually break a barracuda record it was with a comparatively small fish, the European barracuda. The place was the Formigas Rocks, a lonely fish-haunted outcrop surrounded on all sides by the vast depths of the Atlantic Ocean, 70 miles out from San Miguel Island in the Azores. To fish these rocks you have to leave Ponta Delgada on San Miguel

The mouth of a giant (82 lb) barracuda.

The head of a barracuda, showing the stream-lined shape.

early, troll on the way out, anchor and fish overnight and travel back the next day. On this occasion our outward journey was unproductive and we fished for shark throughout the night without getting so much as a touch. Close to the rocks, though, we began to catch numbers of huge Bermuda chub. (These fish, which grow to weights in excess of ten pounds, provide incredible action on light rods.) Then as we left for home, I ran out a yellow Kona Head in the hope of taking a tuna or even marlin on the return journey. We had travelled no more than 100 yards when this big lure was taken by what was obviously a small fish. It turned out to be a new record European barracuda, weighing 22 pounds. This was a monster by European standards, but matched against the greater barracuda it was little more than bait. To make matters worse, it had snatched a massive lure on 130-pound class tackle which gave it no opportunity to fight. Interestingly, once again yellow was the killing colour.

My impression is that truly big barracuda are now rapidly becoming rarer—the days when one could go out and almost guarantee fish of over 40 pounds seem to be long past. Commercial over-fishing and the resulting decline in suitable bait fish has taken its toll. Perhaps there are still places in the world where giant barracuda live and flourish. I hope so. But nowadays when I fish barracuda I work on a catch and release basis.

Mexico. A late evening barracuda for the author. Good barracuda are often taken by trolling with a large Kona Head lure. If in doubt, use one with a yellow skirt, as barracuda seem unable to resist yellow.

4
Mexico

Fishing the Jungle Creeks and Lakes

South of the lovely island of Cozumel, the coast of Yucatan runs in an unbroken line of soft golden sand backed by a forest of majestic coconut palms. Behind lies the province of Quintana Roo, with its scrub and raw jungle. The first break in the line of palms comes at Tulum, the only known example of a Mayan city built on the coast. Tulum is architecturally superb and its walls, temples and civic buildings are almost perfectly preserved. I was fortunate in that I was able, while on a fishing expedition to Yucatan, to spend time at Tulum under the guidance of a Mayan Indian called Esteban who was well-versed in the history of his people and who fascinated me in particular with his interpretation of the city's wall paintings.

Esteban was also my invaluable fishing guide during my stay in Quintana Roo province. Fifty or more miles south of Tulum, at a place called Boca Paila, lay the specialist fishing camp where I stayed. The camp consisted of a superb club house, an outside bar, a huge barbeque pit and a series of well-appointed bungalows, each designed to accommodate two people. It catered mostly for American bonefish anglers, but Esteban soon showed me there were plenty of other fish to be caught, some of them extremely large. The camp is situated on the edge of a vast area of salt-water lakes, creeks and jungle rivers. The jungle around the camp is mixed, but close to the water mangrove trees are predominant. Fish and mangroves seem to go hand in hand; the intricate root system of the mangrove provides food and shelter for many kinds of fish. At Boca Paila small tarpon, snook sting ray, snapper, barracuda, bonefish, permit, shark and the great cubera snapper could all be found in close proximity to the mangrove swamps.

On my first day at the camp, I intended to spend the morning and early evening bonefishing, the perfect way of getting the feel of the place. The afternoons were deemed too hot to fish, so while the guides slept the anglers had time to write letters or logbooks and make plans for the early evening fishing. Already at the camp when I arrived was an ex-Gurkha officer, Tony Watson. Tony had come all the way from Birmingham and was determined to get his money's worth by fishing an 18-hour day. On my first morning he was up at first light fly casting the beach directly in front of the fish camp. On his return he admitted to catching nothing, but I was so taken with his enthusiasm that I offered to share my boat and guide with him.

With a solid breakfast inside us we left the jetty at 9 o'clock and headed at 30 knots up a wild jungle river towards an area where Esteban was sure we would find bonefish. Thirty-five hair-raising minutes later we shot out of the narrow winding waterway into a vast salt-water lake. As we crossed this expanse of water we saw an incredible number of huge sting ray that flapped out of our path. At one point, where the water looked to be around eight feet deep, the bottom was paved with black, ugly sting ray, some even lying on top of others. 'Muy malo' said Esteban. I shared his feelings. A big sting ray is an ugly customer and anyone swimming or wading in these ray-infested waters would

Author with fine houndfish, caught from the beach on light-ish line at an atoll in the Gulf of Mexico.

Deserted beach, good fixed-spool reel and balanced rod. The long clear stretches of sand at Yucatan are a dream for those keen to fish from the shore.

be courting rapid disaster. I have caught enough sting ray all over the world to know how dangerous the long whip-like tail with its mucous-covered serrated-bone spear can be.

At the far side of the salt lake we came to an area of young mangrove, more of a swamp than true jungle. Here the water was so choked with snags that Esteban could not use the outboard and was forced to pole the flat-bottomed skiff through the obstructions. At times he had to get out of the boat to pull and push us through to open water. Twice we tried to join him to give him our help, but on both occasions he waved us back into the boat, obviously acting on instructions received back at camp. I suppose he was right. Had Tony Watson or I been speared by a sting ray it would have meant being airlifted to the nearest hospital, which was over a hundred miles away in the

The Mayan ruins at Tulum. Photograph taken on a fishing trip.

Beautiful African Pompano taken off a beach in Mexico.

66

town of Merida. Esteban himself was presumably regarded as expendable. Finally we emerged into a scene of incredible beauty. In the distance a lone Mayan temple shimmered white in the morning sun; all around us flew brightly coloured parrots and multi-hued kingfishers. Soon we came to an area where natural springs bubbled through the lake bed. Here we began to fish.

We had brought fly and spinning rods, but Esteban advised that the water was too murky for fly casting. I flipped a jig out to the centre of the area of disturbed water, had an instant strike and brought in a small barracuda. Behind me I heard Tony strike and turned to find him hooked into his first bonefish—not an enormous one, but large enough to tear line off in typical bonefish style. With both these first fish safely netted we were eager to find bigger game. We had some time to wait. Twice we saw vague, fleeting

A beautifully conditioned permit for a visiting angler.

A good cubera snapper for fisherman Nick Cranfield at Boca Paila, Yucatan, southeast Mexico.

68

shadows in the silt-clouded water. They were certainly fish, but of what kind I had no way of knowing; they were too big to be bonefish. Esteban thought they might be horse-eye jack and if he was right I knew we would be in for some action. Soon afterwards Tony had a strike which practically lifted him out of the boat and a fish shot out of the dirty water and hightailed it across the shallow flats at speed, taking line like a bonefish. 'Permit', grunted Esteban, 'long fight now.' Reeling in, I sat back to watch Tony battle it out. With the rod hooped hard down he looked at first to be in full control, but the permit had other ideas—using its shield-shaped side to maximum effect it started to

Saltwater flyfishing for bonefish and jacks off a deserted Mexican beach. Standard flyfishing tackle can be used for what is a very satisfying and unusual way of fishing.

Grouper taken on a boat off the Mexican coast.

The dracula-like teeth of a cubera snapper.

kite round in a great half circle, taking out line steadily as it went. With over a hundred yards of line already out Tony could do little to stop or even slow down the fish. To shorten the distance between us and the fish Esteban started to pole the boat after it and for a while these tactics worked—Tony gained around fifty yards of line and we had the permit in sight. The trouble was that if we could see the fish, the fish could see us—and it disliked what it saw. It streaked away at a speed that none of us could believe, almost as if it had changed into a higher gear. This time it made no mistake; it simply powered on until the reel spool was totally empty and the inevitable breakage occurred. Fortunately, the line broke at the knot on the lure—fortunately, because a fish with a small lure in its jaw will usually survive, whereas a fish dragging several hundred yards of line has no chance.

After this disturbance we took no more fish. We set off back to the camp and as we hurtled back down another mangrove-bordered salt river I was able to talk to Esteban about the possibility of other fish. The bonefish were too small for serious interest, the permit too rare to waste time on; what we wanted was some fairly instant action. Esteban said that the deep winding waterways teemed with big fish—shark, barracuda and cubera snapper. It was this last that interested me. Reputed to reach weights in excess of a hundred pounds, it was reckoned to be one of the hardest fighting fish in Central America. Esteban said there were plenty of big ones in the tangled waterways, but that our best chance was to slip over the bar of the Boca Paila outlet and fish in the open sea close to the beach.

So, late that afternoon, we set off—armed with heavy spinning rods and an array of the largest, most brutal-looking plug baits I have ever seen. Each plug was deeply scored by teeth marks, which Esteban told us were made by giant barracuda and huge snapper. I believed him. Earlier that day I had seen a 12-pound cubera snapper brought in by another English angler; small though it was it had a set of vampire-like teeth that would have made even Dracula happy. Arriving at the Boca Paila outlet we found the water so shallow that we had to manhandle the boat over the last hundred feet or so into the deeper water, but beyond the sand bar the water dropped instantly to a depth of around thirty feet. Esteban informed us it was too early to expect cubera, and suggested that we try for barracuda by trolling large plugs astern of the moving boat.

Knowing how barracuda seem to be attracted by yellow-coloured baits, I chose a big multi-hooked yellow-bodied plug that bore little resemblance to any living fish. And, sure enough, it had been in the water no more than a few minutes when a ten-pound barracuda took it. Minutes later, Tony had a fish of about the same size and I got a bright 15-pounder. By this time the light was beginning to go and Esteban told us it was cubera time. Apparently these huge snappers spend most of the day lurking in underwater caverns, emerging at dusk to indulge in a lengthy bout of murder and mayhem. The favoured haunts of the local fish were directly off Boca Paila Bar, where a lively surf and ingoing fish traffic kept them amply supplied with victims. Neither Tony nor I had ever caught a cubera so we had no idea what to expect if we hooked a fish. Initially I thought we were over-gunned in choice of tackle; later I realized our 30-pound class outfit was in fact too light. The first strike came to my rod, after about half an hour of abortive trolling. Whatever sort of strike I had been expecting, it was not this—the fish took so slowly and solidly that I assumed I had snagged a rock; one second I was retrieving, the next everything went solid. Cursing my luck and thinking that I was going to lose an expensive plug bait, I swung the rod sideways in the hope of freeing the hook. Instantly the snag jerked back and I realized only then that I was into a fish. The cubera was totally unimpressed by my actions. It turned very slowly out into the open sea, for a second or so it took line, then, as I increased power and the boat bow swung round to follow the cubera, it simply began to tow the boat out to sea. 'Big one', said Esteban needlessly. For a while the huge fish just pulled our bows in whatever direction it chose to go. It did not seem to be panicked in any way and I certainly had no impression that it was beginning to tire. I played it for some thirty-five minutes; then, abruptly, we parted company. At first I thought the line had parted, but as I started to wind back the loose line I felt the dragging weight of the plug. Finally, as I lifted the bait into the boat, I could see how the fish had freed itself. Two sets of huge trebles were crunched out of shape, one set was totally twisted and broken. The fish had clearly been hooked on the tail set of trebles. Its powerful jaws had worked on the other two sets, crushing and distorting them beyond recognition, and finally it had simply torn itself off the tail set. Bitterly disappointed, we decided to fish on in the hope of contacting another giant snapper.

Esteban recommended a switch to natural baits—'No more strikes on plugs,' he said with conviction. He cut off the remnants of my mangled plug and in its place tied a huge well-sharpened single hook on a wire trace. He rigged Tony in the same way. Then he produced from the bait locker a three-pound bonefish and cut it in half to make two baits. I got the head section, Tony the tail. We simply cast our bait out and let it sink to the bottom, where the tide rolled it round close to the bar mouth. Five minutes later Tony's rod slammed down as somewhere deep down a big fish snatched at the half

Hooked up on a tough-fighting cubera snapper.

Netting pilchards for bait before going after big cubera snapper.

bonefish. The fish fought in the same ponderous manner as its predecessor, slowly pulling the boat after it as it moved across the sea bed. It was obviously puzzled by the constant rod pressure. For a while it would head out to sea, then it would turn and angle back to the dubious security of the bar mouth. By this time a splendid tropical moon had risen to paint a silver wash over the beach and palm trees and shed a shimmering light on the waves that rolled and foamed over the bar. So bright was the moonlight that even tiny details stood out plainly. I could see a fallen palm further along the beach; there was a flicker of movement as some nocturnal animal ran along the water's edge. 'Margay!' Esteban cried, and explained, 'a spotted jungle cat'. I would have liked a closer look at the animal, but Tony's fish was surging out to sea again. For an hour the fish continued to plough around without showing the slightest sign of exhaustion. Finally, an hour and ten minutes after hooking up, Tony lost the fish. This time the hook was intact, but a tiny piece of gristly flesh caught up behind the barb told us what had happened. Time and constant rod pressure had caused the hook to wear a large hole in the snapper's jaw. Finally the hook had simply dropped out, leaving the cubera free to swim away, probably still totally bemused by the whole business. We could hardly believe our bad luck—two very big fish hooked and lost in one session.

It was time to head back for a late snack and a drink or two. Later, when we discussed the fighting ability of cubera snapper, we came to the conclusion that these great fish had strength and endurance well beyond their physical size. We also had the impression that they were somewhat dull-witted—under constant rod pressure they were content just to plod ahead, relying on strength alone to gain them their freedom. Naturally we talked also of our next night's fishing, but our plans were frustrated by a rising wind which remained constant for the remainder of our stay and made fishing in the bar-mouth area an impossibility. Esteban was unworried; he knew another place haunted by great fish. We could spend the morning fly fishing for small tarpon and then, after siesta, head for what he called 'the bay of big fish'.

In fact we discovered next morning that Boca Paila tarpon were not that easy to find. In the end, however, we sighted in a shady corner of a salt flat a shoal of half a dozen fish weighing between 10 and 30 pounds. They lay in a tangle of mangrove roots. A couple of them, we were distressed to see, had flies dangling from their lips. A tarpon fly is large and crude and is designed, on the hairwing principle, to look like a small fish.

To get close to tarpon is to spook them, so we loaded our reels with shooting-head lines and planned to use double-haul casting to gain additional distance and enable us to stay well away from the shoaling fish. Once mastered, a shooting-head line performs miracles and I gained extra length from a stiff breeze at my back. My first cast dropped the long orange-white fly a yard beyond the fish. I knew instinctively that it would produce a take. Sure enough, a fish detached itself from the shoal, sped forward and nailed the lure. Hooked tarpon indulge in instant aerobatics and this fish was typical—the second it felt the hook it broke water in a climbing jump which had to be seen to be believed. Crashing back through the surface film it reappeared instantly in a bouncing frenzy of white water that totally scattered the other shoal members. Then it took off in a reel-screaming run out across open salt flats

Westward TV winner with permit and fine bonefish. The simplicity of the fishing boats can be seen.

into a slightly deeper channel, where it bounced up and down like a rubber ball and whipped the water to foam. It was not a particularly big fish—I reckoned it weighed around 15 pounds—but like all tarpon it fought like a demon. Finally, however, the fish was worn down—more I suspect by its own aerobatics than by my skill or constant rod pressure. Boca Paila tarpon are always released and as I brought it alongside I held it steady to admire its shape and huge silver scales. Seconds later the hook was out and the fish was finning gently away. After this we searched for more tarpon, but in vain; it soon became obvious that the fish had scattered.

On the way back for lunch and the afternoon siesta we stopped in a narrow creek to take several small bonefish and a couple of mangrove snapper on fly rods. Lunch was typically Mexican—locally shot white-wing dove served in a

spicy chocolate sauce. Not all the visiting anglers seemed to enjoy it, but I found it good. After my exhilarating tarpon fight I could have eaten a Mexican donkey—hide and all. The afternoon rest period was spent sorting out tackle ready for our assault on Esteban's 'bay of big fish'. Four o'clock found us down at the jetty 'loaded for bear' with heavy spinning rods, large fixed-spool reels, and loads of line and terminal gear. Esteban's bay turned out to be a great stretch of salt river opening into a jungle-fringed bay full of calm, almost motionless dark water. The place screamed of fish. Esteban tied up to a bunch of giant reed and at that moment the surface of the bay exploded as thousands of terrified bait fish leapt to escape marauding predators. The jump-

A grunt taken on a light line off the Mexico-Belize border. Grunt make fine livebait for barracuda.

78

ing fish ranged in weight from ounces to pounds and it was obvious that some of the attacking fish were quite large. The carnage went on for several minutes, then the surface of the bay became tranquil again. Ten minutes later the process was repeated, giving us the opportunity to study the attack pattern. The predators obviously swept in from the main flow of the river, herding packs of bait fish into the pond-like bay. The bait fish were then cornered against the mangrove roots and reed beds and systematically slaughtered. According to Esteban large barracuda were mainly responsible, but a few huge cubera snapper tagged along to mop up dead and damaged fish left behind by the fast-moving barracuda. There were also sharks, huge fish of undetermined species that spent their entire lives hunting inland salt rivers. Some of them, said Esteban, reached weights in excess of 200 kilos. At the time I didn't believe him—although I was later to change my opinion. We had no live bait, but we did have plenty of bonefish which we chopped into sections to make baits that we cast out well away from the boat. We used no leads to anchor these cut baits; our gear was simply a rod, reel, line and large hook attached to a wire trace. With baits out we sat back and waited for the first strike. Two hundred yards below our position a second boat was fishing in a similar way. An angler in this boat had the first take. We were alerted by a huge splash and the scream of a reel ratchet and looking downstream we could see the angler in the bow position trying desperately to hang on to a giant fish. As we watched, the fish cleared the water completely and I could see it was a barracuda—not the average 10 or 12 pounder but a huge fish in the 30-pound range. Despite maximum pressure and good tackle the angler lost it after it had run over 200 yards and found sanctuary in dense reeds on the opposite bank. Later, I was to see the unlucky angler's reel fingers—burnt and blistered in his vain attempts to slow the fish down. Soon after this fish was lost something picked up my bait and streaked off down river so fast that the line leaving the reel spool became an indistinct blur. Unfortunately whatever it was ejected the bait before I had a chance to strike. Ten minutes later I had another take, but this time the fish slowed down after an initial 40-yard dash and gave me time to set the hook. Once hooked the fish began to jump and run, showing itself to be a big barracuda. I was using a powerful rod and large fixed-spool reel loaded with line with a breaking strain of 18 pounds—tackle that would surely enable me to take a 30-pound fish (as I guessed this one to be) in minutes. The barracuda had other ideas. At first it tore downstream in a vain attempt to break free by power and speed alone; then it turned and came up river so fast that the line hissed as it cut the surface water. Try as I might I couldn't wind fast enough to keep in contact with the fish. A slack line is always dangerous where big fish are concerned and I was convinced that I would lose this one. Fortunately, it suddenly changed direction and tore off across the main river channel, a move which rapidly used up the slack line and put me back into full contact. Barring accidents I now felt confident of being able to beat and ultimately boat the barracuda. Sure enough, in a ten-minute spell I had it circling slowly in towards the gaff. Esteban, an old hand with the gaff, took the fish into the boat with one precise pull. It was a long, lean, racy-looking fish with huge teeth, and I was right—it weighed just on 30 pounds.

Only minutes later Tony had a bite from something which took just a few inches of line at a time. When finally he decided to strike at it he found that it had run back under the boat. Winding like a maniac, he walked the line round the boat's stern—and found himself in solid contact with something which shuffled off through the mangroves into the jungle! The line was out of the water. Tony pulled hard and 50 yards inland some living creature went berserk, flinging immature bushes into the air. Esteban's reply to my suggestion that he should wade ashore with the gaff had best remain unrecorded. We never did find out what Tony had hooked, but it was large, powerful and excessively bad tempered.

High winds roaring in from the sea put paid to our hopes of fishing next day. We waited in vain for the wind to drop for several days, then Tony had to return to England and I had to fly on to Walker's Cay in the Bahamas. I shall return, though, to Yucatan.

5
Bonefish
From Florida Keys to Southern Africa

Zane Grey, writer of Westerns and deep-sea fisherman, once described the bonefish as related to dynamite and chain lightning. I recall being much impressed by this description when, as a child, I borrowed Grey's book *Big Fish* from a London library. In those days, living in bomb-scarred central London, I dreamed incessantly of Grey's accounts of battles with bonefish, although at that time I had little hope of ever experiencing at first hand the speed and courage of a hooked bonefish. Then, nearly thirty years after first reading Grey's book, I found myself aboard a two-seater plane heading down Grand Bahama Island to the world's number one bonefish camp, the Deepwater Cay club. Established by American fisherman and photographer Gil Drake, Deepwater Cay is a Mecca for the world's top anglers. Their quarry is that elusive silver queen of the coral flats, the bonefish.

My Bahamian pilot deposited me on what was no more than a jungle airstrip and as I watched the little plane take off for its return journey to Freeport I looked around expecting a welcoming party. Nothing. Just a rough open area of grass surrounded by mangrove swamps over which magnificent butterflies hovered and assorted water birds passed in dazzling displays of natural splendour. I had nearly an hour to wait before an ancient tractor, driven by a more ancient but charming Bahamian, arrived to collect me, but there was so much to see that the time passed quickly. We were soon at Deepwater Cay, which consists of a clubhouse and a few bungalows where guests sleep and keep their fishing tackle. The Club fronts on to a white sand beach; behind it is the wooden jetty from which the bonefish boats depart. I had arrived too late to get in a full day's fishing but in the afternoon I went out for a three-hour session which produced a couple of mangrove jacks and a small barracuda, but no bonefish. I was disappointed but Frank, my guide, reassured me; tomorrow he said, I would certainly get my bonefish.

Next day with my head crammed with bonefish talk from the night before, I rejoined Frank after an early breakfast and soon the skiff's big outboard engine was speeding us through the waterways to an area of flats where Frank was convinced we would find fish. A bonefish flat is something special—a vast area of shallow water whose bottom is made up of white sand and coral marl interspersed with clumps of brown weed. Many of these flats dry out completely at low water. The bonefish come in with the returning tide, sometimes

John Ablanalp wading the bonefish flats with his guide in the Bahamas.

in shoals, sometimes in pairs, often singly. Their silver bodies show only as grey shadows over the dazzling white bottom. Sometimes their position is given away only by their shiny white tails sticking out of the water as they stand on their heads to root for crabs and other crustaceans hiding in the soft silt of the bottom. I have always had 'fish eyes' but it took me a whole morning to get my eye in and learn how to 'see' bonefish. Because the water was unbelievably clear I assumed that there would be no difficulty in seeing any fish that came within range. I was wrong. Several times I saw smoky shapes in the water, but they came and went at such speed that I assumed them to be nothing more than a stir of current movement. Frank assured me that I

had seen fish; 'Plenty bonefish here, mon,' he told me, obviously exasperated by my inability to see the obvious. Then things changed. 'Bonefish,' he whispered, for perhaps the tenth time, 'Bonefish, 30 yards at 12 o'clock.' Even as he said the words I realized that at last I was seeing fish—three clearly defined bonefish moving purposefully from right to left across our bows. The cast was an easy one, the weight of the prawn itself being enough to flip the bait and hook a yard in front of the leading fish. Instantly all three fish surged forward and I felt a strangely vibrating tug on the line. I struck instantly, set the hook solidly into the taking fish and then stood amazed as it sped off on a hundred-

yard dash which took only seconds to complete. The spool of my spinning reel turned so fast that it was little more than a blur from which rose a whiff of blue smoke as the friction heated the oil on the reel spindle. Now I appreciated what bonefishing was truly about. I had caught many fish in my time—giant blue marlin, huge tuna, ten-pound trout and a host of other notables—but I had never come across a fish that ran as fast and as hard as this bonefish. I have no idea how long I fought it. All I can remember is its speed and its ability to change direction. It made run after long run before finally allowing itself to be drawn over the rim of the sunken landing net. Its weight was just five pounds. I could not believe that a fish as diminutive as that could have fought such a

A bonefish on line being brought in over the flats. Bonefish camouflage is so good that often it is a matter of the angler sensing their presence rather than seeing them.

Dawn over Deepwater Cay Club, Grand Bahamas.

long fast battle against full rod pressure and eight-pound test line. Frank just laughed. 'Wait till you gets a big bone, mon,' he said.

Two fish later it was time to quit, but by that time I had both a raging bout of bonefish fever and high plans for the next day.

Next morning I fished with a new guide. I had lost Frank to a party of regular customers who flew in that night and asked for him as their guide. His replacement was a young man called Willis Monroe, whose home was on one of the Abaco Islands on the outer edge of the Bahamas. I had just come from a billfish tournament in the Abaco chain and because of this Willis and I became instant friends. Twenty years old, he had been acting as a bonefish guide for only four seasons, and as the youngest and least experienced of the local guides, he was fish hungry. He had something to prove, and that, matched with my newly developed bonefish fever, made us a formidable partnership. It was true that I was a beginner—I had had only one full day's bonefishing in my life. But I had some advantages. An English angler, used to hard-fished waters, has a better chance of catching fish than probably any other angler in the world. On the rivers I fished at home each fish had been caught and released many times. Here on the lovely bonefish flats few fish had ever felt a hook. English casting techniques were also superior. I had long since learned to cast light baits a long way without forfeiting accuracy. My first day's bone-fishing had also showed me the limitations of the short casting rods that are traditional in the United States and the Bahamas. I felt that a longer rod would give me more casting range, a better chance of hooking taking fish and fuller control of running fish. Fortunately, I had with me an 11-foot English rod. The American anglers thought it hysterically comic and dubbed it 'the English clothes-pole' and even Willis had his doubts.

That first day with Willis was fascinating. 'Get comfortable,' he said, 'We gwine run two hours.' That two hours took us first through a maze of creeks out into the open ocean and then inshore again to run at high speed into what appeared to be solid jungle. Seconds before impact with the land seemed inevitable, Willis throttled back and swung the boat into a tiny gap in the mangrove thickets. It was the entrance to a creek that we followed for over half a mile, emerging at the throat of a mighty expanse of shimmering flats. This was Big Sound, an aptly named expanse of perfect bonefish water totally sheltered from the open sea and fringed on all sides by coral and jungle. The bird life was prolific and so tame that it was possible to pole to within feet of nesting herons, pelicans and a host of lesser birds. I only wish I had had time to photograph and study the birds of Big Sound but we had come in search of

Author with fine 10½ lb and 9½ lb bonefish at Deep-water Cay, Grand Bahamas.

bonefish and with the fever running high nothing else truly mattered. Big Sound was thick with bonefish. In the first hour I took five fish ranging from three to six pounds. My long rod behaved perfectly, the additional casting distance it gave being enough to take fish which Willis reckoned to be well out of range.

Lunch, which we took around midday, was interrupted by my sighting a tailing bonefish. I cast to it and caught it. I also saw several other bonefish which came so close to our position that I was able to photograph them as they searched the bottom for food.

Lunch over, we had just poled across an inlet channel when an 80-pound shark appeared. The moment Willis saw it he wanted its jaws to give to a girl

90

friend. Hooking it was easy. I simply flipped a prawn bait in front of it and struck the instant it sucked it in. Small shark may be dour and sluggish fighters in open deep water, but hooked in two feet of water they can put on a turn of speed that has to be seen to be believed. Our fish made only one long run, then it stayed about thirty yards from the boat, refusing to come any closer. Willis said that shark always did this and that the only way to finish the fight was to get out of the boat and walk up on the fish. It sounded crazy to me, but I had caught many massive sharks on the high seas and this one did not look too aggressive, so I was prepared to give it a try. What followed would have been hilarious to any spectator. Every time we got to within gaffing range of the shark it charged directly at the nearest pair of legs. Whether this was an intentional effort to attack or simply a defensive action I have no way of knowing, but it kept us hopping about in a constant spray of water and churned-up coral marl. Finally, however, it was over and Willis had his shark.

With the fish safely inside the boat I cut a few yards of chaffed line off the reel and tied on a new hook and we headed away from the clouded water in search of more bonefish. This time we ran into a shoal that, we agreed, must have contained close on a hundred prime bonefish. They were middle-weights, the largest weighing around 8 pounds, the smallest around 3 pounds. Opening the bale arm of the reel, I flipped the prawn bait a yard ahead of the moving pack and watched fascinated as the fish surged forward en masse to intercept the bait. I hooked-up, but to which fish I had no idea. Still, I

Two good bonefish taken on flyfishing tackle.

expected that the hooked fish would reveal itself by abandoning the shoal and making a break for open water. For all I know it may have tried, but wherever it went the whole shoal followed. Whether it turned right or left, the whole shoal turned as one fish. For the next ten minutes I played a vast shoal of one of the worlds most sought-after fish. The pack only deserted seconds before Willis slipped the landing net under a nice five-pounder.

Minutes after we had returned the fish to the water we found the same shoal again. This time, to conserve baits, I switched to an artificial lure—a bonefish jig with a triangular metal head behind which a coarse fibre tail partly covered a large plaited hook. It was a pink-headed monstrosity, and, although I had read a great deal about the effectiveness of this type of jig, I had little faith in it. But from a caster's point of view it was a winner. Because of its lead-coated head it could easily be dropped in front of fish cruising at the very limit of normal casting range. Another advantage was that bonefish obviously saw the tadpole-like jig as some sort of natural food. Often they hit it within seconds of my starting to retrieve the lure, and in this way I took a number of nice fish. The trouble was that I lost even more. The jig definitely had fish appeal, but its poor design made it bad at hooking the fish. The hook was so coarse and thick

Bonefish with typical markings over coral marl. The markings blend so well that to an inexperienced eye the passing of bonefish can look like nothing more than a stir in the current.

Bonefish country, near Deepwater Cay, Bahamas.

A fine bonefish being taken from the landing net.

in the wire that no amount of sharpening really improved it. Nonetheless I ended the day's fishing with 14 fish under my belt.

I was back at Deepwater Cay in time to get myself a rum-and-coke from the clubroom bar and sit outside to watch a typically magnificent Bahamian sunset. When news of our 14-fish catch became general knowledge everyone wanted to see and handle my much-maligned rod. The best American bag that day had been three fish, so my 'clothes-pole' had proved its point; anglers who had scoffed at its length now coveted custom-made versions based on blanks ordered from England. Then someone brought up the subject of fly casting for bonefish and within minutes I had accepted a challenge to leave my bait pole home and go out after bonefish with a fly rod. I had read much about fly fishing in salt water and had brought a fly-casting outfit with me. Taking a 'bone' on fly tackle was the ultimate thrill according to the aficionados at Deepwater Cay, so I hardly needed the bottle of Scotch that someone wagered against me to make me determined to try my hand. Under protest I bought a selection of American bonefish flies, all of which were clumsily tied on hooks far too thick in the wire. I had shown my own selection of home-tied English patterns—Leaded Shrimps, Jersey Herds and a large version of the popular Copper Nymph. The American anglers looked at them and delivered their verdict: good enough for stock-pond trout but a waste of time on the wily, discerning bonefish. By this time I was beginning to understand these bonefish specialists and their attitudes. They love to put down other anglers' tackle, whose bad points they will discuss at great length: but they clam up the moment their own ideas and gear are mentioned. They would rather die than give away their own secrets. All this is part and parcel of bonefish madness. I should know. I had as bad a case as the next man.

The following morning Willis eyed the fly rod with misgivings. He had hoped for at least another double-figure day, because that sort of success would increase his standing with visiting anglers, the other guides and the camp management and might lead to pay rises and a chance to take out the big tippers. But it was generally acknowledged that big catches were rare on fly tackle, two or three fish being a good yield. However he took the boat through the creeks cheerfully enough, apparently heading back to Big Sound. When we came out into the open sea I expected him to turn and run along the coast. Instead he increased the engine speed and hammered straight on out to sea. 'Where are we going?' I yelled at him. 'Little Mangrove Cay' came his

Bonefisher Willis Monroe with 6 lb fish at Little Mangrove Cay, Bahamas.

A deserted Caribbean beach, typical of the angler's dream conditions.

reply. Nearly three hours later I saw ahead a low mound of an island thick with lush green mangrove trees. Turning in behind the island Willis cut the motor so that we drifted into a flat that appeared to boil with questing bonefish. I could count dozens of tails and see groups of fish in all directions. 'Nobody don't never fish here,' Willis said—and I believed him. Little Mangrove Cay had its problems. Projecting everywhere above the water were the straight-tipped shoots of mangrove roots, each one capable of breaking a taut line in seconds. Still, with all those bonefish in sight I had to give it a try, although I doubted that I would land any fish I hooked. To begin with I tied on a true bonefish fly, a weird-looking shrimp variant which incorporated bead eyes and a sludgy brown chenille body wrap. It did not look much to me but it must have looked good to the cruising bonefish. In less than an hour I had hooked six, one of them a monster. I lost two fish because mangrove shoots cut the leader; the other four shed the hook within seconds—the nine-foot fly rod just was not powerful enough to set the crude hook to which the fly had been tied. Finally I had had enough. I abandoned the true bonefish flies and switched to a large version of the Jersey Herd tied on a long-shank No. 6 Partridge hook. Willis was appalled. 'Wrong fly for this place,' he said. 'Well, maybe,' I thought, 'but worth a try.' With the fly line piled on the platform at my feet I waited until I saw a largish solitary fish feeding in a comparatively free area of marl. Double-hauling to gain distance, I placed a fly a yard beyond the fish, gave it a second or two to sink, then began to retrieve in short, slow spurts. The bonefish must have seen the fly as it began to move across its path. One second it was grubbing about on the sea bed, the next it lunged forward, soaked up the fly and began to run. The weight of the line alone was enough to set the fine wire hook. I hung on in grim amazement as the fish made the big reel scream. The backing splice went through the rod rings in a second and it was not long after that I realized that my 150 yards of backing was running dangerously low. By a miracle the fish had chosen to run out into slightly deeper water and with Willis poling fast we were able to follow it out into a relatively snag-free area. I have caught many fish on fly rods, but I had never known a fish of this size to generate such power. A fly rod is a hefty piece of equipment and dragging a No. 8 line and over a hundred yards of backing through the water should have been more than enough to slow this fish down. But it was so strong that it seemed to ignore the spring of the rod and the drogue effect of the line. Nonetheless I was confident of bringing the fish to the net once I had worked it clear of the mangrove shoots. It seemed firmly hooked and I had plenty of time to play it out. Finally the fish was finished. It was a plump eight-pounder. I weighed and returned it as quickly as possible.

I went on to take four more fish. Willis was delighted—five fish boated was a good day's fly rodding which could only help to improve his status at camp. I was elated but exhausted. My arms felt as though they had been stretched on a rack and my back muscles ached as though I had fought a big billfish. Back at camp, I collected my bottle of Scotch and showed off the English trout flies that had caught the fish. I particularly relished pointing out the difference in the hooks and explaining how the thick wire of the orthodox bonefish fly had caused me to prick but not truly hook a number of fish.

Good as my day's fishing had been, I had learnt from it that the fly rod had definite limitations in snagged-up water. Some of the Little Mangrove Cay bonefish had been huge but they had been feeding among the mangrove shoots where I could not get at them. So I planned to go back next day with a long bait-casting rod and a reel loaded with 15-pound B.S. line. Willis was not at all certain that this strategy would work. He thought that no bonefish would stop to pick up a bait presented on such a heavy line. So, to keep him happy, I agreed to take with me a conventional bonefish outfit that I could turn to if the fish refused baits on heavy tackle.

Little Mangrove Cay was a long way by any standards but with a flat calm sea the outboard motor could be given full throttle to send us planing over blue water at a rate of 30-plus knots. After nearly three hours the low outline of the Cay appeared and within a few minutes we were easing into the bay where we hoped to find bonefish. The water was alive with tailing fish. Taking up my position on the bow platform of the boat I waited as Willis deftly poled the skiff into the jumble of projecting mangrove shoots. We had already agreed that this would be a big fish or nothing day. It was my last day at Deepwater Cay and I wanted a bonefish over ten pounds in weight. Few bonefish anglers ever manage such a fish, but having seen so many big fish the previous day I felt I was in with a chance. With the skiff barely moving both of us watched and waited for a sight of a heavyweight. Fish of up to about six pounds were everywhere but at first there was no sign of the larger fish. Bonefish, however, have a habit of materializing out of nowhere. I was looking at a large empty area of coral marl when right in the middle of it a big bonefish suddenly appeared. Moreover, it was feeding—even as I watched it put its nose down into the silt-like marl and began rooting for food. The cast was an easy one—a simple flip of the rod top to drop the prawn a foot or two in front of the fish. Now we should see if I was right about using a thicker line.

I need not have worried. The second the bait hit the water the fish moved ahead to intercept it, and as I saw the prawn vanish into its mouth I struck hard and far back to set the hook as solidly as possible. Like all bonefish this one took immediate evasive action, making the clutch on the reel scream as it tore off line. Although I could apply much more pressure than normal, I made little impression on the frantically running fish. Then, with over 75 yards of line out, the fish swung round in a huge arc that dragged the taut line across dozens of projecting mangrove shoots. Even with the thicker line a breakage seemed inevitable, but in fact the heavy nylon line simply flattened the shoots as it swept across them. Twice more the fish tried the same tactic and twice more the line withstood the test. Finally it became obvious that the fish was weakening and soon the battle was over. The fish was in the net and we could see that it was obviously over the magical ten-pound mark. More than eight hours later it was officially weighed in at 10½ pounds. When first netted it would have weighed close on 12 pounds, but during those eight hot hours it had become dehydrated and lost a great deal of weight.

With this first big fish in the boat I wanted another. Within ten minutes I saw a second hefty fish feeding at the root of a mangrove shoot. Again it was an easy cast and within seconds the fish was hooked and running. By now I knew the line would hold and this gave me the confidence to bully the fish. Later that second fish weighed in at 9½ pounds. Having caught my brace of big fish I now fished on a hook-and-release basis, taking nine other fish during the day. Back at Deepwater Cay my two big fish came in for a great deal of comment and several anglers who were staying on asked for Willis as their guide. I was told that my two big fish would probably be permanently displayed in the clubhouse, but as I have never returned to the Deepwater Cay Club I cannot say whether they are still there.

Waiting on the tiny airstrip the following morning it was hard to believe that I had finally turned my boyish dreams, kindled in the grimy bomb-torn streets of wartime London, into reality. But it was true. The bonefish flats so vividly described in Zane Grey's book are now permanently etched upon my mind; the blue water, the white coral sand and the splash of feeding bonefish are held now in my memory as well as in my imagination.

6
Orkney Game
Midnight Lochs and Steel Grey Sea

Night sky over Hundland Loch, at one o'clock in the morning.

Early summer sunsets in Orkney set the lochs and hills aflame with splendour. I remember spending a magical week in a tiny croft on the shores of lovely Hundland Loch in late June, a time of year when the sun set only for a few minutes. In the brief twilights I cast fly to the fish that dappled the loch surface as they rose to suck in the tiny insects hatched on the marshy shoreline. Hundland could not have changed much from the time the first Vikings stalked the valleys and hills of Orkney—only my temporary home and a distant farmhouse were new to the scene. In my isolation I had time to drink in the beauty of the hills and to listen to the lovely call of distant curlew.

Harray boatman John Gaddie holding a beautiful brown trout from the Loch of Harray, Mainland Orkney.

Orkney is an angler's paradise. It is a land of splendid lochs, all of which contain trout. Hundland trout were small by Orcadian standards—three-to-the-pound brownies that fed boldly and fought like fish twice their size. For me Hundland was just an after-supper water. My days were spent on Harray and Swannay, where the trout grow larger. But I looked forward to the after-supper hours that I spent casting either from a gently drifting boat or, to trout feeding in inches of water, from a shore carpeted with marsh marigolds. Hundland fish I always returned to the water, grateful for their spirit and beauty.

Harray was different—a vast spread of water where giant trout were known to exist. It was a loch of dense weed beds, rock-strewn skerries and deeps where trout lurked in water as amber-coloured as good whisky. Most visiting anglers stayed and fished from the hotel, but I preferred to live in isolation beside lovely Hundland. Every day I drove down to Harray, along moorland roads beside which redshanks guarded their nests and chicks, with short-eared owls flying overhead on silent wings. For me the 30-minute drive was both part of the anticipation and a kind of pilgrimage that prepared me for the fishing day ahead. I would arrive to find my boatman, John Gaddie, waiting for me, seated as always on the gunwale of the clinker-built loch boat. In typical Orcadian manner, John liked to start the day as he would later end it—with a generous nip of whisky. Once whisky-warmed, he would and could row all day. He knew every inch of Harray's vast acreage like the back of his hand. Fishing was his passion and his knowledge of Harray trout was supreme. He knew all the feeding areas, knew the trout's habits at a weather change and always he could put me on to fish.

Traditionally Harray is fished in 'loch style', which means short casts and a three-fly leash—one fly deep, one higher and one just working the surface film. My south-country upbringing made it difficult for me to feel confidence in such methods. My preference, much to John Gaddie's horror, was to use a single fly and a long cast to find fish. Worse still, in John's view, was my habit of using south-country flies in preference to local patterns. The top local fly was a black Ke-He, a pattern originally tied to imitate a long-vanished bee-like fly which apparently haunted Harray until the end of the 1930s. I believe that an angler fishes best when he has full confidence in his fly. To me the Ke-He, particularly the blue variant, looked like nothing on earth, so despite John's misgivings I stuck to tried and trusted patterns—mainly shrimp imitations and the green-wool version of the damsel-fly nymph. Of the two patterns the damsel fly, worked through the weed and rocks on a slow-sinking line, was the killer: the Harray trout took it as violently as any south-country rainbow.

I recall one lovely fish taken from a winding gully in a barely submerged rock skerry. With John holding the boat deftly in position I cast a long line to drop the fly softly into the deepest section of the gully. Pausing to let the fly sink, I began to retrieve line jerkily, hoping to imitate the movement of a natural insect. The trout took almost immediately, slamming into the fly so hard that it set the hook on impact, and turned instantly in an attempt to regain the shelter of the nearby rock wall. Harray trout seldom jump; they occasionally roll in the surface waves but mostly they stay deep. This fish was

Two typical Orcadian trout, with rod, reel and sinking line.

Scapa Flow close to Burray, with the Isle of Hoy in the background.

typical. It stayed deep, confident in its ability to break free, so, although I knew it was a good fish, I had no way of knowing its weight. I was prepared, though, for a four-pounder and was surprised when the fish that finally surfaced was less than half this weight. I suppose I should have known better than to assess a Harray fish without sighting it—all Orcadian trout fight far beyond their weight. Watching it slide over the rim of the landing net I found myself comparing its lean hardness with the softer-looking fish of the Hampshire chalk streams. This trout from the windswept Orkneys was a product of its unforgiving environment. Food does not come easily to these loch fish. Each morsel has to be searched for, hunted out and taken before some other

A beautiful small brownie, showing the markings, typical of Orcadian trout. This one was taken on an old fashioned wetfly.

fish snatches it away. Chalk-stream fish do not have to work to eat. They simply pick a prime position and wait for the river seasons to provide them with a constant supply of waterborne insects. Theirs is the millionaire life, the river working ceaselessly to satisfy their appetites, tantalizing their jaded palates with mayfly, caddis, sedge and hawthorne until eating becomes little more than a habit. Slipping this Orkney fish from the net, I gently eased the hook from its jaw and leaned over to release it, watching as it regained its balance and tail-waved its way back into the depths. I could sense my boat-man's amazement. He was used to visiting anglers who took their catches back to the hotel for display on dishes. I could see the attraction of this traditional display of success and skill, but I had no need of this fish and no one to display

Three beautifully marked loch trout.

John Gaddie holding three typical Loch Harray trout.

Trout are not the only prize from Orkney: a superb 192 lb common skate being brought to the surface. My preference is for a matched 50 lb outfit with a full set of AFTCO roller rings. Trimmed coalfish makes a good bait.

it to. Besides there is a subtle satisfaction in catching and releasing a beautiful fish that no amount of land-based admiration can hope to match.

Few Orkney days are totally windless, but occasionally in the evening the wind will abate long enough to create calm conditions and it is then that the lochs come alive with rising trout. My special memories of the Orkney lochs are of times like these, when dancing waves slap gently against the clinker hull of the rowboat. Fly hatches come suddenly on Orkney lochs. Many times, after I have been casting mechanically for several fruitless hours, a subtle shift of wind has brought a fly hatch tumbling over the surface. Instantly the trout come up, splashing savagely in the short waves. This is a time of excitement. Usually the trout are not selective; they are up to feed, and anything that looks

like a hatching insect will be taken. Under these circumstances I change to a black-and-peacock spider and cast not to specific rises but simply into areas where the action is thickest. Takes are usually decisive, the fish seldom coming short to the fly. Only very rarely does an excited trout slash at a fly without actually taking it. This boiling activity seldom lasts long. The duration of the rise may be only minutes, and it is up to the angler to make the most of such occasions.

I remember one rise on Loch Swannay, when the activity centred in the exact area I was already fishing. The fly itself was little more than a tiny dark midge, yet those Swannay trout came up as eagerly as a Test trout after mayfly. It seemed to me that the fish were taking mouthfuls of insects rather than individual flies. My black-and-peacock spider looked huge in comparison to the natural insect, yet it was invariably taken within seconds of touching the surface film. The rise lasted for close to thirty minutes, and I managed to take two brace of trout while it lasted. I also lost what I fondly believe to have been the largest Orcadian trout I have ever hooked. My only sighting of this trout was its neb breaking surface as it gulped down my semi-waterlogged fly. It

Bringing the skate into the boat. Fish of 200 lb + are known to exist off the coast of Britain and Ireland: one commercially caught fish weighed in at 400 lb.

was little more than a cast length from the boat when it rose and as it turned down I was able to set the hook solidly simply by raising the tip of the fly rod. Initially I was confident that I would land the fish but it reacted violently to the jag of the hook, running out and away from the boat at high speed. Within seconds it had run out all my fly line and had started to take out backing as well. This was the first time an Orkney brown trout had treated me in this way and I made a mistake. Had I been fishing the loch of Stenness I would have assumed the fish to be a fresh-run sea trout. Here on Swannay I knew it had to be a brown and piled on pressure accordingly. My cast had a breaking strain of only three pounds, but this had been strong enough to hold four splendid trout and I was sure it would hold with this great fish. To begin with things went my way. The fish reacted to rod pressure and slowed to a halt. For a second or so it was stalemate. Then the fish began to slap the taut leader with its tail. Whether the leader had a flaw, or whether I held a fraction too hard I shall never know, but the leader broke and my great fish was gone, trailing a yard of nylon and with my black-and peacock spider firmly set in its iron jaw. I was sorry to lose this fish; it was a trout that even now I dream about. Its weight? Who knows? In my mind it grows larger by the year, a dream fish from a place where dreams are made and sometimes fulfilled.

But there is more to Orkney than trout fishing. Miles of rugged coastline, savage tides and isolated islands make it a sea angler's paradise. From the great cliffs of Hoy Island come cod and ling, pollack and coalfish and occasionally huge diamond-shaped halibut. This is an exciting place to fish, for the tides that sweep down past Marwick Head surge and roll round the feet of the Old Man of Hoy in a never-ending swirl of white water that sets the sea birds flying and the salt spray rising like a grey mist on the cliff face. Atlantic seals abound in this area, often appearing beside the fishing boats as living proof that the sea beneath the keel is alive with fish. I have fished off Hoy Island on many occasions, mostly from a boat called *Girl Shona* whose owner-skipper Michael Flett earns his living catching lobsters from the rough grounds around the islands that make up the Orkneys. Michael is a fisherman descended from generations of fishermen. His knowledge of the sea is second to none and never has he failed to put me on fish.

Oddly enough I have never caught one of the Orkneys' giant skates when fishing with Michael. He is essentially an open-sea man. The skate prefer more sheltered waters, such as Scapa Flow—in two world wars a busy haven for ships, now a graveyard of rusting hulks. Scapa Flow is now a peaceful inland sea, where huge bat-like skate move morosely over the sea bed in a ceaseless quest for scallops, clams and crabs. Skate fishing inside the 'Flow' is always an exciting business. It is also a slow pastime that gives the angler plenty of opportunity to gaze and wonder at the green treeless hills of Orkney or at the rusting remnants of a once-proud navy. Orkney is steeped in history. Since men first took to the sea Scapa Flow has provided a safe harbour. When the Vikings first came to Orkney the Flow must have sheltered many longships, some of which no doubt still rest beneath its deep waters. Certainly many Viking sailors lie buried with their armour and possessions in known and unknown graves on the green rise of land that practically surrounds this mighty natural harbour.

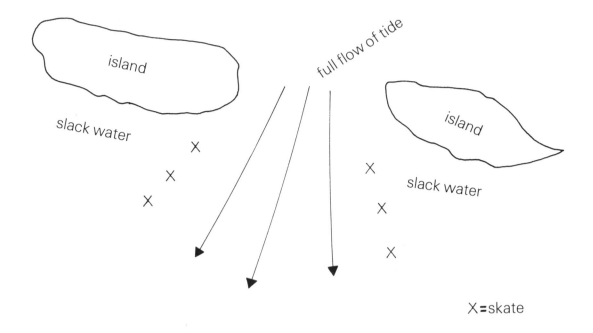

island

slack water

full flow of tide

island

slack water

X

X

X

X

X

X

X=skate

From a fishing point of view Scapa Flow has a great deal to offer. Shore fishing produces flatfish, small coalfish and mackerel. Many a night I have fished at midnight from the Churchill barriers built in World War II to prevent U-boats entering Scapa Flow. These barriers, which link south Ronaldsay to mainland Orkney, are a fine place to spin for mackerel. These are plump northern mackerel that fight like fish ten times their size—fine fish to take back to the home croft to be cleaned and gutted, rolled in oatmeal and fried for breakfast. Occasionally the flashing spinner will attract a bonus fish, a high-leaping sea trout that makes a welcome addition to the larder. Orkney is a wild place and, although it boasts some plush restaurants, it seems fitting that you should cook your own catch, perhaps to eat with fresh-picked mushrooms in front of a peat fire in a tiny croft.

Boat fishing inside the Flow can also be good. Huge pollack can be caught by trolling along the rugged island cliffs. The Triton Bank is thick with cod and ling, and giant common skate can be found at any point within the Flow. No one can say for sure how large common skate grow. I have caught them to 192 pounds in Orcadian waters and much larger fish are known to exist. Most of these great fish are very old. I have heard it said that it takes them more than sixty years to reach a weight approaching two hundred pounds. Whether this is true or not I do not know, but I know that the giant skate I have caught have all given the appearance of great age. They had a prehistoric look about them, these great winged wonders brought up from the eternal darkness of deep water for their first and possibly last-ever sight of daylight. Once boated

Skate prefer slack water on the edge of a main run of tide. The flow of the water provides a plentiful supply of food.

they lay on the deckboards like humped table tops, their large eyes partially covered by a strangely frilled eyelid-like membrane. There was a time when most anglers automatically killed any large skate they caught and brought it ashore for a symbolic weighing ceremony, in the hope that it would weigh more than one hundred pounds and so qualify them for membership of the 'Ton-up Club'. Today's more conservation-conscious anglers return the majority of giant skate alive to the sea. This is one reason why skate still thrive around the Orkney Islands. Like most anglers, I have in the past killed giant skate. Now I return each one I catch, for I know that my satisfaction lies not in the kill but in the recollection of battle as I walk at the end of the day, my shoulders still aching, through the crooked streets of Stromness or Kirkwall. The pleasure I take in my victory is enhanced rather than diminished by memories of that moment after the battle when I watch the released skate wing its way back to its silty home far beyond the reach of daylight.

Trout from the lochs and skate from the Flow ensure that the Orkneys deserve a place in any angler's dreams. But there is one other fish that makes a

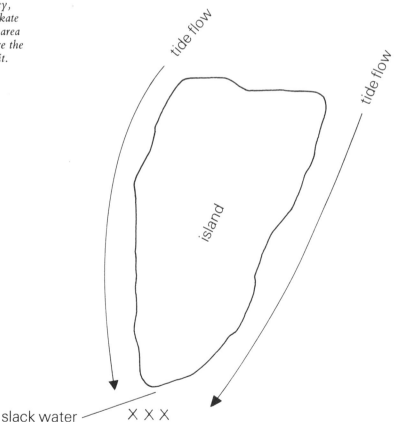

Typical skate habitat, found in Scapa Flow, Orkney, where one of the best skate marks lies in the slack area behind an island, where the tidal flow has been split.

trip to Orkney something special. That is the sea trout, caught not in rivers (for there are none) nor in the lovely Loch of Stenness, but in the sea itself. Wherever a tiny spill of freshwater drains across a shell-scattered beach big sea trout may collect by the dozen. Attracted by the smell and taste of fresh water, they have one urge—to claw their way upstream and lay their eggs on the river-washed gravel where the fry will grow until they in their turn feel the call of the open ocean. The adult fish collect impatiently beyond the surf, waiting for a summer rainstorm to turn their chosen rivulet into a raging waterway large enough to give them passage. While they are waiting they fall readily to lure or fly. Orcadian anglers traditionally spin for these fish. I prefer to fly fish, not because I think this the more productive technique, but because to cast into the angry white water and to feel the electrifying take of a big sea trout is a magical experience. I have ineradicable memories of standing waist deep in surf, with my powerful reservoir fly rod hooped into a great fighting arc, as out in the foam-flecked water a great sea trout heads for deep water and safety.

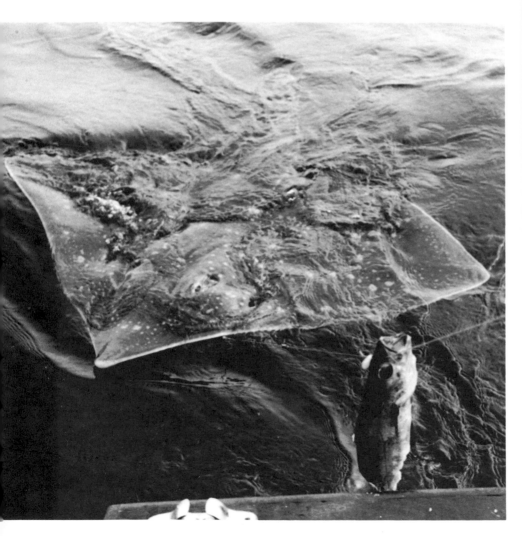

A fine 158 lb common skate comes to the boat. These— sometimes called grey or blue skate—are found in good numbers in both Irish and Scottish waters.

Drift fishing from the stern off the Old Man of Hoy.

Losses are invariably high in this style of fishing. The sea bed is strewn with knife-edged shells, which can cut through a taut leader like scissors through paper. Two out of three hooked fish are lost in this way.

There are, of course, other ways of losing sea trout. I remember fishing late at night below Burray village on an occasion when my blue-and-silver fly was intercepted just before it disappeared into the white-water surf. The taking fish was obviously large; it ran line out swiftly as it headed into the bay. But I had ample backing on the reel and my only fear was that the leader would part. For a while all went well; although the fish was still fresh I felt it begin to give ground and for the first time I was able to gain line. Then, just as I felt confident, the line went slack. I cursed my luck, my cast and whatever shellfish was responsible for my loss and started to wind in the slack line. I had retrieved about twenty feet when I realized I was still hooked to something. It did not feel like a sea trout—there was no dash, no fire, no rod-jerking rush, just an inert, but living, weight. Had I been in the tropics I would have assumed that my fish had been taken by a cruising shark, but this was the cold northern sea of the Orkneys. Still, there was something at the end of my line cruising slowly from right to left in front of me. Then abruptly, the water erupted and there gazing at me with dark, knowing eyes was a seal, with the dead sea trout clamped firmly in its whiskered jaws. For several seconds we looked at one another in total disbelief. Then the seal gave a snort, shook its head (snapping the leader in the process) and sank slowly out of sight. It did not reappear and knowing that presence would scare off every sea trout for miles, I decided to call it a day. I felt no anger. The seal had more right to the fish than I had and I was grateful that I had been vouchsafed the sight of such a splendid animal at such close quarters and in such circumstances.

It is now some years since I visited Orkney. Hopefully I shall be going back soon. Those lovely northern isles have their own kind of magic—a magic steeped in ancient history, freedom, good fishing and island hospitality.

7
Reef Fishing
Battling with the Exotic

As a child I eagerly watched television films shot by the pioneer underwater photographer Hans Hass and promised myself that one day I would dive, and more importantly fish, over the life-filled reefs that Hass's camera revealed. Because I watched on my parents' fuzzy black-and-white television set, I had no idea of the variety of colours displayed by reef fish, seeing only an area filled to overflowing with fish of all shapes and sizes. But that monotone view was more than enough to set me dreaming.

For me, the dream first approached reality in the Seychelles, where I quick-

Strawberry grouper from a reef off Florida. These boldly patterned fish are found all round the Caribbean.

ly discovered that a reef is a thing of unbelievable beauty. Unfortunately I was making only a brief visit and although I was able to dive on several occasions I had no opportunity to fish. So I had to wait for several more years for my first taste of reef fishing, until, during a trip to Nassau in the Bahamas, I was invited to fish over a series of shallow inshore reefs and submerged coral heads.

I was surprised and fascinated by the pure clarity of the sea. The boat was anchored in about 35 feet of water, but every stone on the sea bed showed in sharp relief. Our gear was simple: light rod, small lead weight, wire trace, standard bottom-fishing hook and fish bait.

When my bait reached bottom I felt a pull and thought for a moment that I

Two kinds of snapper from a coral head in the West Indies.

Canadian angler on a fishing holiday displays his fine Bahamian grouper.

A mouth-gaffed grouper brought aboard off Walker's Cay, Abaco Islands, Bahamas.

had hit a snag; then the 'snag' took off on a heavy run which tested the light tackle to the limit. Looking round I saw that all four anglers in the boat were stuck into fish of varying sizes. Mine turned out to be a hefty brown-and-gold grouper. The other anglers had between them a brace of yellowtail snappers and a bright red strawberry grouper. With these fish unhooked and stowed in the well we rebaited and, instantly, hooked up on a second batch of bright and varied reef fish. On the third drop I set the hook into a lively fish which subsequently turned out to be a queen triggerfish—one of the prettiest of the

Deep-water reef fish from off the Atlantic Islands. At the depth at which these fish live, their striking colour fades out completely.

Fine wahoo being boated over a reef.

A silver scabbard fish, one of a variety of ultra deep-water species found over reefs throughout the Atlantic.

Wahoo often bite short, behind the tail of a deadbait: the two hook rig helps prevent this.

world's reef fish. Pausing only to photograph and return my catch I quickly got back into the action. Never in my life had I experienced such fast fishing. At the end of the first hour most of us were beginning to weaken and all of us had hooked unseen monsters which had casually snapped our light lines. Twice I lost yellowtails to good-sized barracuda, and once I had a large grouper chopped in half by a reef shark. Yet we had anchored over an area where there was no sign of fish; not a shadow or a flicker of fins moved against the clearly discernible sea bed. That there was a lot of marine activity became

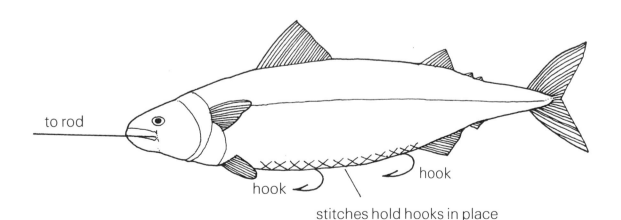

to rod

hook

hook

stitches hold hooks in place

Weighing a large grouper.

Queen trigger fish from Mexico on a light line; these are found throughout the West Indies.

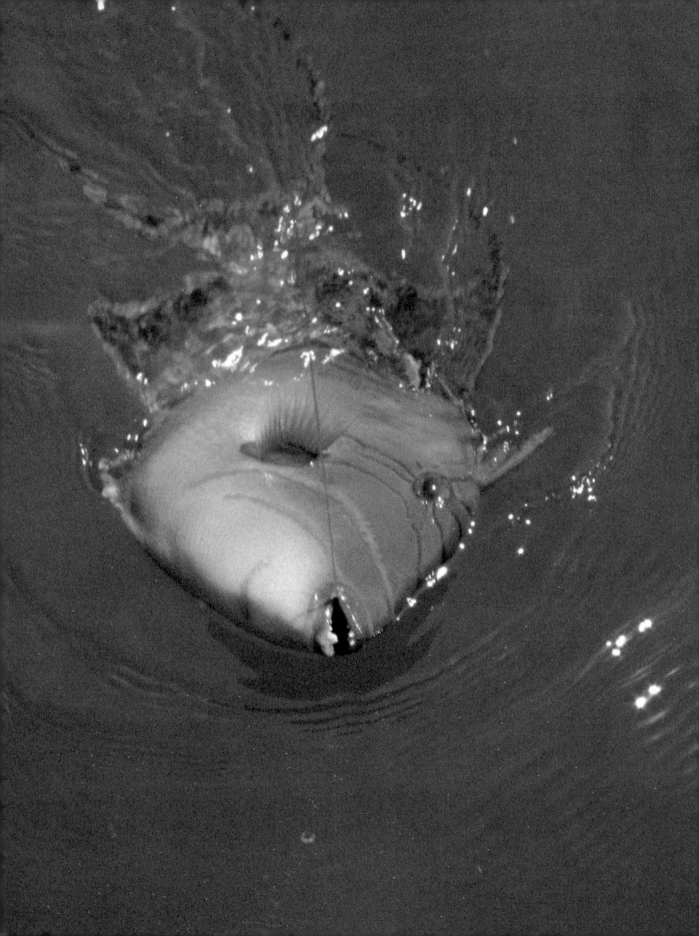

Bringing aboard a dolphin in the Bahamas: note the size of the Penn fighting reel and the way the butt of the rod fits into position.

obvious the second a bait touched bottom, but even then we could not see the fish until they began to fight. Later, as I travelled around the Caribbean, I got used to the invisibility of reef fish, but on this first occasion I found it puzzling and mysterious.

I much enjoyed this my initiation into reef fishing, but we had fished a comparatively shallow area and I soon found that deeper waters offered still more excitements. I was introduced to deep-water reef fishing off Walker's Cay, aboard Bob Ablanalp's magnificent sport-fishing boat, *Sea Lion II*. Bob is a fanatical reef fisherman; give him a light outfit and chum up a batch of yellowtails and he will play for hours. But he is no big-game fisherman; go out deep sea on a marlin trip and he will come as a spectator but probably not bother to fish. (Which, incidentally, creates a problem, because if Bob is not fishing he will be playing host all day—which means providing the anglers aboard with an endless supply of rum-and-coke.) On my first deep-reef expedition, however, Bob was out to fish and the bottle stayed stoppered. First stop was a shallow inshore mark where we took a number of small groupers which we carefully unhooked and stored in the big live-bait well under the decking. Then, when skipper Bob decided that we had enough bait, we raised anchor and headed out for deeper water. We stowed away our light rods and made ready a selection of 20- and 30-pound class rods. We used much the same terminal tackle as on the inshore reefs, except that the hooks and traces had been beefed up accordingly. The graphic sounder showed that the water was around 150 feet in depth; its print-out displayed the sea bed as a chaos of high peaks and deep canyons. Our plan was to drift with the tide to allow the baits to cover plenty of ground. Our tackle losses would obviously be high, but the rugged underwater terrain of coral rock looked more than capable of producing some hot fishing.

A hog-snapper taken off the Bahamas; note the distinctive teeth.

With a small live grouper on each hook we lowered away until we felt the lead touch bottom. Everyone else on the boat knew what to expect, but I had no experience of this sort of fishing and the first bite came as something of a shock. The bait was taken with no preliminary warning—something big,

strong and fast-moving simply swam up and swallowed it. Once second I could feel the lead bouncing across the rock, the next the rod was arched over and line was ripping off the reel spool at high speed. There was no question of not hooking the fish; the bite was so definite that the fish was hooked on impact. Knowing the perils of fishing over snaggy rock, I put the pressure on to raise the fish from the bottom. Initially it lifted easily, finning up out of the depths without too much resistance. Suddenly, it realized its danger and power-dived back to the sea bed. Constant rod pressure soon had it back on the move and after a 10-minute battle it was wallowing alongside the boat. It was a big amberjack. From its appearance I reckoned that it weighed over 40

Gaffing and boating a medium grouper off Florida.

A large grouper on a yellow lure, Indian Ocean. Grouper also like oily-fleshed bait fish, such as mackerel or bonito.

pounds—a good fish by any standards and a nice start to deep-water reef fishing. Bahamian amberjack are dangerous to eat, so we let this one go—rather than kill it the mate snipped the trace close to the hook and the fish disappeared into deep water.

With a new well-sharpened hook attached, another small grouper was sent down to take its chances over the fish-filled coral. When the next bite came I knew immediately that I had hit a monster. The bite was a simple slow surge that dragged the rod down to an unbelievable angle. 'Big grouper,' the mate confidently diagnosed. It was more like fighting a slow-moving truck than a living creature. Try as I might I could not induce the fish to come off the sea bed, in fact I felt that it had not even noticed my efforts. Finally it moved off into cover and everything went solid. 'Giant grouper,' said the crew, 'they always behave like that—probably didn't even know it was hooked.'

Gaffing a big grouper on the island of Madeira. Big grouper seldom venture more than a yard or so from cover and once hooked rush for their stronghold. The perfect tackle for the job is an 80 lb class rod, with reel to match.

Gaffing a fine Nassau grouper.

*Florida coast. A good-sized
amberjack.*

*Miami angler, off Florida,
proudly displays his beautifully
conditioned grouper.*

Wreck fish taken over a reef in the Atlantic. These come up as far north as Britain but are rarely taken.

While I was repairing the damage to my terminal tackle Bob Ablanalp's son John hit a nice lively fish which ultimately turned into a long, lean mean-looking barracuda. So it went on; we caught a lot of fish but kept losing the big ones.

Finally, in an effort to raise just one really huge grouper, we tied a heavy trace to an 80-pound I.G.F.A. outfit and baited it with a three- or four-pound grouper. Big grouper are cannibals, preying for the most part on the massed packs of small grouper that infest every coral reef. We thought that this bigger-than-average live bait would soon attract the attention of one of the ever-hungry monsters lurking beneath our keel. We were right; within five minutes something had found and swallowed the bait. The mate had the rod and he quickly slid into the fighting chair and clipped on a shoulder harness. But, whatever the fish was, it put an incredible strain on the heavy gear; the mate could do little to lift it. We all had the impression that it was totally oblivious of hook, line, rod and angler and was continuing, unperturbed, to ease over the sea bed in search of food. It must have been of vast size. No matter how hard the mate worked he failed to raise the fish. Finally, the inevitable

133

happened, and it went to ground in some coral cave.

So the day went on. We won some battles and put some hefty fish in the boat. We also lost a good many fish, all of them big. Finally, we ran out of live baits and turned to a different technique, that of deep jigging with artificial lures. The lures were made of lead moulded round the shank of a big hook, and each jig was tipped with a brush of stiff white nylon bristle. The technique was to drop the bait down to the rock, wind up a few turns and work the bait by raising and lowering the rod tip. The grouper took the bait hard, usually hooking themselves on impact, and we managed to boat a number of nice 20- to 30-pound fish. Sadly, though, the jigs seemed of little interest to the monsters. Next day, Bob Ablanalp took us to a very different kind of reef. This was the wreck of a Spanish treasure ship, the *San Juan Evangelista*, which one stormy night foundered with all hands in the comparatively shallow waters of Great Bahama Bank. The treasure, if it had ever been there, had long gone, but the wreck was still in reasonable condition and alive with fish of many kinds. After several hundred years under the water the ship had become the core of a short barrier of reef, which should produce some excellent fishing. Big amberjack were our main target and we also had a chance of

A green wrasse, such as is found through the West Indies. This one was taken in the Bahamas.

Beautiful mahogany snapper, taken off the Virgin Isles, Greater Antilles. These fish are found throughout the Caribbean.

Reef life is murder and mayhem. This fish was taken already at a meal.

finding a cobia. Never common, cobia apparently used the old wreck as a temporary base on their travels across sand.

Having been brought up on stories of the Spanish main and books like *Treasure Island*, I was fascinated by the thought of fishing over the wreck of a genuine, well-documented Spanish galleon. True, I had once before fished a Spanish treasure ship—the *Valenserra*, off the northern Irish coast—but the *San Juan Evangelista* rested in tropical waters, which made it more romantic and more appealing.

Once *Sea Lion II* arrived in the wreck area, the skipper ordered the mate to break out part of the boat's anti-pirate armament and fire directly into the water. Personally, I thought he had gone crazy, but moments after several shots had been fired into the water up came a batch of curious turtles. Apparently these creatures sleep in the wreck and rise at the vibration of gunfire, so establishing the exact centre of the wreck.

Because we were fishing such shallow waters we could use weightless tackle, simply tying a hook and trace to the main reel line. Bait was frozen squid, used whole, which we dropped over the stern of the boat and allowed to drift back and down to where hopefully the big fish waited. Oddly enough the turtles stayed on the surface to watch our every movement, making no attempt to swim away.

Moments after dropping our baits we hit fish—big scrappy amberjack that fought like tigers for every inch gained. This was purely sport fishing; we had no practical use for the fish so each was played out, assessed and released to live and fight another day. Throughout the day the turtles waited and watched—

A beautiful grouper caught deep jigging in the Bahamas.

presumably after we left they breathed a sigh of relief and dived once more to sleep among the Spanish dead.

Since then I have tried my luck on many reefs throughout the world. Invariably the fish are plentiful, brightly coloured and hard fighting. Often species overlap—grouper of one sort or another have a worldwide distribution. Some fish, however, stand out beyond all others. My favourite, for fighting ability and superb colouring, is probably the queen triggerfish. I am fascinated too by the African pompano—a fish which changes its shape and fin structure many times before reaching maturity. I have caught pompano only over reefs off central America; its burnished-silver colouring makes it as beautiful as the queen trigger.

Reef fish come in such a range of shapes, colours and habits that an angler could spend a lifetime fishing the world's reefs and come across only a fraction of the living miracles that inhabit them. The chance still exists of catching a specimen of a totally unknown species. I am sure that the seas still hold fish unknown to science, perhaps around Madagascar, over the same reefs that have yielded coelacanth. So the world's reefs are still magical places. Certainly I shall never regret or forget the reefs that I have fished, where multicoloured fish of many kinds took every bait dropped to them and where the coral reefs provided an enchanted underwater arena for days of unparalleled sport.

8
Shark

Man's Ancient Foe

Gaffing one of the author's record white tip sharks. Until 1980 no white tip shark had been encountered on rod in European waters, although it is common in tropical seas.

As a child I used to holiday in the little port of Mevagissey in the West of England. It was then and still is a picture-postcard place, although now, unfortunately, it is saturated with tourists. When I spent my summer holidays there the war was still a near memory and mass tourism was a thing of the future. The only real visitors to Mevagissey were anglers, mostly shark anglers. Day after day I would be at the harbour to watch the shark boats come in and to see the carcasses swung up and weighed on the dock-side. In a child's eyes a 100-pound blue shark is a monster, a creature to fire the imag-

The author's son with a large
blue shark. A 50 lb class rod
and multiplier reel should be
used for a fish such as this one.

A porbeagle being boated.

Author fighting hard against
a white tip. The white tip
shark is a known man-eater.
At around 7 feet the examples
from the Azores are at the
upper end of the scale: the
average being 4–6 feet.

ination. I became obsessive about sharks and began to study and read as much about them as I could.

When I was 14 years old I spent my entire holiday money on a single day's shark fishing. I forget the name of the boat and of its captain, but every other detail of that first shark encounter is indelibly printed on my mind. I remember that the weather was bad that summer and that for days the boats were unable to go out. I had booked my trip and paid my money, but I was dreadfully afraid that I would not get to sea before the time came to go home. Fortunately the sea gods smiled and with only two days left before my holiday ended I went out for the first time. In those days blue shark were the mainstay of the Cornish shark-fishing industry, which meant that we had to fish about fifteen miles out. Cornish shark boats have never been fast and it was some two hours later that the skipper announced our arrival on the fishing grounds. After so many days of bad weather, the sea was still quite rough and conditions not at all promising. Four of us were to fish, each sitting by a rod. At the end of each hour we were to change places, the idea being to give every angler a chance in the best position. Nothing happened during the first hour. Nothing happened during the second hour. The wind, however, was getting up and

540 lb mako, from Fayal.

142

A hooked mako shark charges the boat. Mako are common in the Atlantic, and should be fished for with an 80 lb rod with full roller rings and matched reel and lure.

our skipper warned us that we might have to stop fishing and head back to port. I was as desperate as any 14-year-old could be, I had saved and planned for this opportunity, now it looked as though the weather would cheat me of the chance to catch or even see a live shark.

Suddenly the whole situation changed. The heavy rod beside me dipped and the great Fortuna reel began to scream as out in the grey waves something big and heavy picked up the bait. With the skipper shouting instructions at me, I picked up the rod, fell into the fighting chair and prepared to do battle. Under the skipper's guidance I screwed down the big brass star drag on the reel and for the first time felt the full weight of the shark. The shark was hooked—but so was I. This was my first-ever encounter with a live shark, but I felt as though I had been fighting fish like this all my life. The battle probably lasted less than ten minutes. I never saw the fish until, finally, the skipper reached over and mouth-gaffed it. Later, it weighed in at 84 pounds; small by local standards, but huge and symbolic to a boy from central London. In those days few people owned a camera, so my first shark was never photographed.

The jaws of the mako in the black and white photograph on page 142.

Jens Ploug Hansen fights a shark from the 'improvised' chair of a simple boat.

144

This fish, photographed in the Bahamas, was destroyed by a shark which attacked it after it had taken the hook.

But I can still see it in my mind's eye—its huge pectoral fins, nictitating eye membrane and wide mouth full of surprisingly small teeth. It was a dream shark that began for me a lifetime pursuit of sharks in every corner of the globe.

Not all my memories are of giant fish; size is immaterial when measured against surroundings and situations. I remember one isolated, unnamed beach in central America. Offshore a great sweep of reef kept the inshore lagoon placid, while behind giant palm trees rustled to the constant sea winds. Far down the coast a vast mountain towered blue-black in the morning sunlight. Close inshore a shoal of big fish worked, scattering the tiny bait fish that teemed in the calm, clear water. I was only on the beach by accident; I had been flying north to Mexico when mechanical failure forced my charter plane to make an emergency landing at an isolated jungle airstrip. Replacement parts would take a day to arrive, which meant that the gods had given me a spare day for some unexpected fishing. I proposed to use a spinning rod to catch a barracuda, then to use a half or a quarter of the barracuda as bait for something larger. I had no shore-casting rod with me, but I felt I could at a pinch cast a big bait on a medium-weight boat stick. Catching the barracuda was easy; I took a five-pounder on my second cast. I quickly cut it in half and chose the head section for bait, carefully positioning the big hook so that its point and barb were not masked by the fish's bony face plates. As trace I had five feet of single-strand wire; I would have preferred twice that length, but knew I would be unable to cast it with a short boat rod. Wading out as far as I could I managed an awkward but satisfactory 25-yard cast that put the big bait out on the edge of a dark, deep channel. By paying out line as I waded back to shore I kept the bait in position; after that I just had to wait. I suppose I expected instant action, but nearly two hours later I was still waiting in a sun hot enough to fry eggs.

Then at last I saw the line lift at the point where it entered the sea; somewhere out on the edge of the channel something had found and was sampling my bait. Twice more the line twitched and fell slack, then abruptly it drew

Mako shark taken in the Azores, where most of the big makos are now taken.

Blue shark, weighing in at 448 lb, caught off Fayal.

taut and I felt the big reel spool turn under my thumb. From the twitchy start to the bite I knew that I had a shark—what kind of shark would soon reveal itself. The fish's slow, steady run turned into a mad rush as it felt the hook point. I pushed the reel into gear and let the fish set the hook itself. Its reaction was instant and impressive. It bounced out of the water in a high, twisting leap that brought it completely clear of the sea; twice more it jumped, each time twisting rapidly in the air. It was a spinner shark and a good one. Now the boat rod felt really short and inadequate: I was almost running along the beach to keep up with the fast-moving shark. It made no attempt to head out to sea. This is not unusual with spinner shark, who live most of their lives in shallow water. Not big by shark standards, the spinner is an active fish capable of putting up a good fight on light tackle. The boat rod, however, was more than a match for it and within ten minutes I had the fish wallowing in the slight surf. The hook was set solidly in the fleshy corner of its jaw. I had no need of the fish and no desire to kill it, so I used my fishing pliers to sever the wire trace as close to the hook as possible. The shark quickly recovered; within seconds it was thrashing its way back into deeper water. It was, compared with many of the big shark I have caught, a diminutive fish, but the circumstances of its capture make it for me a memorable shark. That long, white beach, the palm trees and the distant mountain made a backdrop that I can still conjure up in my memory.

Not all shark catches are enacted in such idyllic surroundings, some come in the vast bleakness of the ocean, far from sight of land, and the battles are

A cruising blue shark. Minutes later it was hooked. Most rod-caught blue sharks are around 60 lb, although the record stands at over 400 lb.

148

fought over submerged banks and the sunken peaks of submarine mountains. Such areas, which can be found in many parts of the world, are normally rich in fish life and they attract shark of many kinds—indeed, one of the fascinations of fishing these remote places is that you can never predict either the types of fish you will find or the methods you will have to employ to catch them. Oceanic sharks are great wanderers who make the world their hunting ground. To seek them out, long-range fishing trips are necessary. These are never easy to organise—and impossible without a certain amount of luck; nine out of ten expeditions are ruined by sudden unpredicted weather changes. When things do go right, however, the fishing can be spectacular.

Record-breaking white tip shark for the author, Azores.

One such shark-hunting trip, which started in the outer islands of the Bahamas, produced amazing fishing. We were to rendezvous with a commercial swordfish boat that was operating more than a hundred miles out, over a deep sunken reef where broadbill swordfish were plentiful. Unfortunately for the commercial men, very few hooked swordfish arrived at the boat undamaged; their struggles attracted sharks by the dozen. The captain of the swordfish boat was unable to say what type of shark was causing the damage— to him sharks were big or small and trouble. These he classified as big, and when he learned of our intention to fish smelly baits in the vicinity of his boat, he gave it as his opinion that we would probably run out of rods, reels and lines in the first couple of hours.

We found the commercial boat and climbed aboard to see for ourselves the sort of damage that was being done by the marauding sharks. We were shown the remains of huge broadbill swordfish whose leathery bodies had been chopped clean through. A big shark can take 60 to 100 pounds of meat at a bite; we saw swordfish from whose flesh vast scallops had disappeared that could only have been taken by monsters. Most of the damage was being done at night, so we began fishing at sundown, lowering the first baits over the side as the sun began to flame the horizon. Bait, of course, was no problem to us; we had plenty of fresh, chewed broadbill flesh available. This looked more like meat than fish flesh, and as each huge bait touched the surface it spread a pool of oily blood, a natural attractant for the hoped-for shark. Fishing just two rods, we set one bait at 250 feet and the second at a little over 100 feet, hoping that one or other bait would find and so establish the feeding level of the night. With the sun gone and the moon on the rise, we settled back to await results. Night on a tropical sea can be unbelievably beautiful. On this night there was a full moon. There was no breath of wind to disturb the slow rise and fall of the sea surface and the only sounds were the gentle creakings of the boat. At a little after midnight a flock of small migrating landbirds passed high overhead and for a brief moment the air was full of their soft music. Soon afterwards the deep-set bait was taken—in a rod-wrenching rush that made the big reel scream. Unfortunately, the fish took the bait but not the hook, but we rebaited and fished on with confidence. Once again the bait was taken, but this time the fish was on the hook. On first impact a hooked shark is impossible to assess; I have hooked huge fish that felt tiny and small shark that felt like monsters. This fish was slow to move, a fair indication that it was big. For a while it cruised gently, taking only a few slow yards of line. Finally it woke up to the drag on its mouth and in typical big-shark style reacted savagely, plunging down in a rolling dive that pulled me half out of the fighting chair. The run lasted only moments before the fish slowed again and levelled out. Shaking its head, it cruised slowly upwards, allowing me to gain line easily. During the next half hour it made two more deep runs, each time taking over a hundred yards of line. When these tactics failed it eased upwards again. Fifty yards astern of the boat it surfaced in a huge flurry of flying white water that sparked brilliantly in the moonlight. The vast disturbance hid from our sight the fish itself. To me it felt like a big tiger shark. Tigers don't have the dash and vigour of a mako or a white shark, but they have the strength of their size and a sort of dim stolidness that makes them fight to the very last. This fish

A mako shark steams in close to the boat looking for a bait. The mako is an Atlantic species that reaches weights of 700 lb and over.

had been on the hook for over two hours before it showed any sign of losing strength. When the end came, however, it came quickly—one minute the fish looked set to fight on, but next it went into a slow death roll. I was puzzled; it seemed too sudden to be right. Then I felt a huge tug on the line, a dragging, snatching jerk that could only be made by one thing—another shark. My killer of the seas was being attacked by another, still more massive, predator.

By this time the boat had come awake; deck lights and searchlights illuminated the water around us. Suddenly my fish was in full view, a great brown dappled shark surrounded by a haze of escaping blood. It was a big tiger shark—probably well in excess of 1,000 pounds. As it came alongside it was snatched down out of sight. For several seconds the water foamed and boiled and the big rod bent and jerked. Then all activity ceased. I reeled into the boat the tattered remnants that were still left on my hook. The fish had been torn apart—from the vent back it had been eaten away, a huge crescent-shaped bite had removed its stomach and at the back of its neck a vast bite mark showed where it had been shaken like a rat. I judged from the teeth marks that the aggressor was a white shark. Whatever it was, it had a devastating effect on that whole area of sea—for two days we saw no sign of shark, presumably because the giant was still on the prowl. Finally, and after an appalling weather forecast, we decided to quit.

My favourite species of shark is the mako. This is a fish that is spoken of with awe in even the most elite of game-fishing circles. Mako shark never reach the weights attained by tiger or white shark, but they compensate in fighting ability for what they lack in length and girth. They are a jumping species capable of a display of temperament that makes even marlin seem placid. Built for high-speed cruising, aggressive by nature and always hungry, a mako travels with its lower jaw slightly dropped to expose its formidable array of razor-sharp teeth.

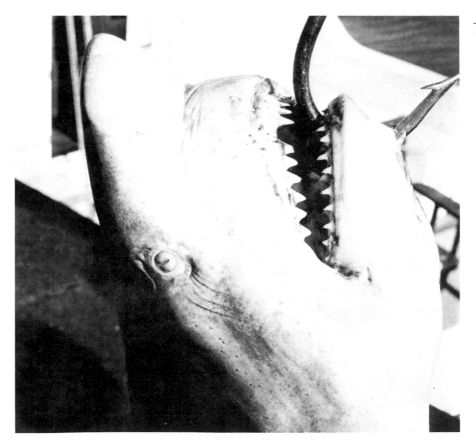

Jaws and tip of the record white tip shark.

Unknown and unidentified spotted shark, possibly a porbeagle mutation, caught by the author in the English Channel.

The first mako I ever saw was a 250-pounder brought into Mevagissey harbour in Cornwall. News of its capture had already spread by radio and the whole fishing community turned out to watch the fish landed for weighing. In a port noted for blue shark the dead mako stood out like a star from a chorus line. Blue shark may look graceful in the water but out of it they look and smell like a sack of garbage. The mako was different, a great hard-bodied fish that even in death looked every inch a fighter. To my young eyes it was a revelation. I had already caught a few blue shark, but they were nothing compared to this magnificent mako. For a whole year I thought of mako and dreamed of taking one. I talked to every shark-boat skipper I knew and managed to piece together a mental picture of mako shark. They seemed to like tide rips and areas adjacent to rocks. They were never common in British waters, but had been known to haunt the dreaded Manacles Rocks off Falmouth. The occasional mako had been caught by anglers drifting for blue shark, usually in the late evening—the local view, in fact, was that they were a mainly nocturnal species. Most of the fish hooked were lost, usually after a long and impressive battle. To a young angler this was heady stuff—I laid plans, made traces and built and strengthened rods against the faint hope that some day someone would give me the chance to fish for a mako. Shark fever is a hard disease to shake off and the Mevagissey fishermen must have thought me mad. Charitably, though, they would tell me of any shark they saw or of any shark activity they heard about.

This was more than thirty years ago, and in those days pilchards were still being caught in vast numbers off Cornwall. These oily fish in turn attracted many shark. One day the captain of one of the fishing boats told me that for two nights running while drifting for pilchard he had lost fish and a section of net to a huge shark which he was sure was a mako. Eagerly I asked if I could go out with him and try to catch the shark. Rather surprisingly, he agreed, on condition that I would lend his crew a hand with their night's work. So, later that bright autumn afternoon, I went aboard his boat, with my tackle made up and a bucket of freshly caught mackerel as bait. Two hours later we had 'shet' the nets and were laid off while the crew made tea. My first bout of fishing produced nothing but disappointment, but when the first haul of pilchards had been dragged aboard and the nets re-set I tried again. We were by then within half-an-hour of midnight and the night was bright, with a full moon. I put a dozen freshly netted pilchards on the hook and waited with all the confidence of youth and inexperience. Twenty minutes later I was still waiting. Then I heard the reel begin to tick slowly over; somewhere out in the dark water a shark was eating my carefully prepared bait. Convinced that the fish was a blue shark, I took up my rod and began to pay out line from my hard-used and many-times-secondhand 'Fortuna' reel. This old winch had seen many better times and many fish; its acquisition had cost me several weeks of hard work on the fish quays, and I was justifiably proud of it. The rod, of split cane, I had built from a kit, fitting each ring and applying each wrap and coat of varnish with attentive love. It seemed to me very bad luck that the first fish on which I tried it should be 'only' a blue shark. I tightened the drag, struck—and found myself fast to a mighty torpedo of a shark that made the reel hiss as it tore off and began to jump. I saw it clearly in the moonlight and realized for the first time that my despised blue was in fact a mako and a monster at that. Hearing the commotion, the skipper appeared at my side. ''Tis a girt big shark,' he said, 'must be that bugger that tore our net to shreds.' The fish was trying every trick in the book to break free—running, jumping, doubling back. I made mistakes. Twice the fish ran back towards the boat and created a huge bag of slack line because I failed to crank the reel handles fast enough to keep pace with it. Then again it ran back, but this time it jumped and fell on to the taut line. No fishing line could stand this sort of treatment; the line broke and the fish was gone. I felt sick to my boots at having lost it, particularly as it would have been, I am still certain, a European record.

Later in life I was to learn that giant mako lead a charmed life—for every

Light tackle sharking is one of the most exciting forms of fishing available.

big mako boated another dozen smash their way to freedom. I have now caught a number over 500 pounds, but I have hooked fish of nearly double this weight and so far all of them have escaped—many simply slipping the hook after minutes of explosive action.

It is not only big sharks that are memorable. One fish I caught off the English coast created a puzzle that has yet to be solved. We were drifting south of the Isle of Wight in an area known to be frequented by large porbeagle shark. The day was fine and the fishing good, and by mid-afternoon we had boated seven large porbeagles, of which I had caught four. But then the fishing slowed to a dead stop and it seemed that the porbeagle pack had moved off. For an hour nothing came near out baits, then, suddenly, I had a screaming run. There were no preliminary indications, just an immediate solid take. Hooking the fish was easy; I simply slipped the reel into gear and the hook set itself. The fish hardly slowed down, and within seconds I had lost more than half the line on my reel. Yelling to the skipper to follow the fleeing fish, I began to pile on pressure in an attempt to turn it. But nothing I could do seemed to have any effect—with the boat running flat out I had trouble gaining even a yard or two of line. By the time the fish did show signs of weakening we had chased it for over three miles. Finally it began to give ground until I had all the line back on the reel. The second the trace swivel snicked up against the top rod ring everyone aboard went into well-practised action with the gaff and tail ropes. Until this time we had not sighted the fish and I had assumed it to be a monster porbeagle. But now we could see that we had caught something very unusual. Porbeagle are normally thick-set fish with an overall grey coloration; this shark was long, lean, and in colour a brilliant silver with a freckling of dark spots. Once the shark was in the boat the burnished silver sheen began to tarnish, but even so it was much brighter than any of the porbeagles we had caught. Stopping only to take a couple of photographs, we turned the boat homeward. In those days all our shark went to a mink farm and when we landed, late in the evening, we routinely telephoned the farmer, waited for him to arrive, loaded all the shark onto his pick-up and went home to eat and sleep. The following morning I realized belatedly that I had disposed of a fish that should have been kept for scientific study and broke all traffic laws driving to the farm in the hope of finding my silver shark still intact. I was too late; the silver fish had been the first off the truck and the first to be cut up. Later I sent the photographs of the shark to the Natural History Museum in London. As a result, I had a long letter from a fish expert there who said that although my fish was obviously closely related to the porbeagle shark the chances were that it was a species new to science and that if I ever caught another specimen the museum would arrange instant collection of the carcass. But, it is perhaps needless to say, I have never seen another.

But I never see a woman in a mink coat without thinking of sharks.

9
Trout

Chalk Stream to River, the Sacred Test

One hundred yards above the junction pool, the tiny river took a right-hand turn beneath a plank bridge. Below the bridge the river had washed out a deep scour, and in this scour lived the largest brown trout I had ever seen. Knowledgeable, like all big fish, this trout had chosen its position well: the pilings of the bridge sheltered it from the flow of fast water and offered instant sanctuary should danger appear. The trout had been familiar for many seasons to the anglers who fished the river. Legend had it that the fish had been hooked on three occasions. Each hooking had followed a similar pattern: the dry fly had landed an inch below the bridge pile, the huge fish had sipped it down and

A beautifully marked trout taken on a floating line.

A typical, hard-fighting Upper Test brown trout.

promptly bolted back under the bridge—breaking the leader like cotton. The last hooking had occurred three seasons before. Now the trout could be seen but not tempted.

The little river was the Dever. A long friendship with the river keeper had allowed me to fish this river and its neighbouring River Test on many occasions. On each visit I asked whether the giant had been caught, and on each visit I tried to induce it to take a fly. Now it was early June and I was back on the river watching the pool for activity. With raft after raft of spent mayfly drifting down the trout must surely feed. No one could be sure how much it weighed, but my guess was that it was more than 12 pounds, and a fish of this size needs a regular intake of food simply to maintain its weight. Hopefully it would rise to the massed mayfly.

For half a bright morning I watched in vain as hundreds of succulent mayfly drifted and danced across the pool. Finally, I wandered off upstream in search of more rewarding sport. By 5 o'clock in the afternoon I had reached the top hatch pool. En route I had taken a brace of four-pound brown trout. I had spent much time casting to the many fine grayling in the river. Always obliging risers, the grayling invariably added interest to my day. Now I decided to retrace my steps through lush water-meadows to sit and wait again below the

An excellent brown trout taken on a nymph.

bridge pool. I was not very hopeful that the great fish would show itself. But old habits die hard and the vigil below the pool had become something of a tradition. On my way back I met my keeper friend who told me that in mid-afternoon the fish had fed hard for ten minutes. This was bad news. If the fish had already fed, the chances were it would stay down until morning. Still, I had a fine brace of fish and it was worth taking a chance that the great brown would make a mistake and start feeding again.

Skirting the pool by many yards I took up a position well below the bridge. Here I intended to sit and watch and wait until the first white owl drifted across the cooling meadows. Below me in a fast ripple a few small grayling fed avidly, each rise ring showing the distinctive bubble left by the fish. Beyond the ripple, where the water slowed and deepened, a good trout rose steadily and confidently. The mayfly had thinned out, but there were still enough to attract hungry fish. For a while I watched fascinated as the distant trout picked off spent mayfly.

The sound of a heavy fish rising in the bridge pool brought back my wandering attention. I had missed the rise, but even as I watched a great blunt

A beautiful trout with the handle of a light split cane rod.

American brook trout, introduced into the River Test at Bossington. Taken on a dry fly.

neb appeared and engulfed a second drifting fly. Straightway I began to false cast, knowing that the fish could stop rising at any moment. The Dever, like most chalk streams, is a split-cane river, a place where cane is hallowed and carbon or glass rods are regarded as infernal machines. I am happy to follow tradition—used properly and with respect, cane comes to life in an angler's hands and my cane rod was as sweet a casting pole as any I have handled. My intention was to drop the spent-mayfly imitation as close to the bridge as possible—a mistake at this stage would put the trout down instantly. The success of the cast depended on luck, concentration and as much casting skill as I could hope to muster. For once everything went to plan; the big fly landed lightly less than an inch from the bridge pile. Instantly a huge nose appeared and the fly vanished from the surface. I knew that if the fish vanished beneath the bridge it would be lost forever and I had long since formed a simple, if unorthodox, plan to frustrate this manoeuvre. Now I put the plan into effect. The second I hooked the trout I bent and picked up a pebble with my left hand and threw it to land directly above the bridge. Instantly, the great brownie turned and bolted down-river—into water so shallow that the fish was practically grounded; it thrashed the water to foam in its desperation to escape. Seeing it fully exposed for the first time, I could only gasp at its size. If ever there was a dream fish, this was it—a monster fit for a glass case. For a split second it stopped its thrashing and I was able to see every dark spot on its vast body. Then, realizing its vulnerability, the fish rolled over, turned its head upstream and made a final perfect run for cover. In hindsight I can see that I should have waded out between it and the bridge, but I had been too busy admiring its shape and markings. Now it was back under the bridge; already I could feel the cast sawing against the water-worn piling. In desperation I waded out to change the angle of the endangered line, but I was far, far too late. As I entered the water the cast parted and my fly line floated down to tangle round my waders. I was shaking so much that I had to stand in the water until the spasm passed; I had lost the brown trout of a lifetime. Only yards from where I stood it was back under cover, its iron jaw clamped firmly down on my mayfly imitation.

During later visits I waited several times for the trout to feed again, but it never did. Later that year it died and its remains, already mutilated by birds and rodents, were found by the keeper. They weighed close on 14 pounds. It must have been one of the last of the mighty chalk-stream brownies—fish that were once common but seem to have been wiped out by increased angling activity and by waterborne pollution.

Today some of the finest chalk-stream fishing is to be had on lesser rivers like the Arle, the Anton and the lovely Wylie. Much of this fishing is in private hands, but much is also available on a day-ticket or club-subscription basis. These little rivers mostly run clear and shallow through verdant banks of lush water-weed, rich in insect life. They hold a good head of fish, most of which weigh less than 16 ounces. A one-and-a-half pounder is an excellent catch, and a two-pounder is a fish to boast about.

One of my favourite small chalk rivers is the Arle below Alresford in Hampshire. There is a day-ticket section on this bright and lovely stream that provides first-class fishing at an affordable price. Like most chalk waters, the

Summer 1986. Author with first brace of double figure brownies to be caught on fly in Britain. The fish were taken from Dever Springs, Hampshire, and weighed 10 lb 4 oz and 10 lb 10½ oz. Both were taken on nymph tied by the author.

Arle is essentially a brown-trout water. It contains a good head of native brown trout—bright little six- to eight-ounce fish that show the distinctive red spots of the wild brown trout. These tiny fish are unsophisticated feeders, eager to snatch at any fly or nymph or rise to a dry fly. I am fond of them because when I was a small boy they, as much as any big fish, were part of my dreams. I lived for a time—a far-off time when the sun always seemed to shine—on the banks of a tiny Devon stream. Acid though it was the stream maintained a good head of wild brown trout and it was these jewel-like little fish that started a boy angler's dreams. Now, when I fish the rippling Arle I often take time to stalk and catch its native brown trout in memory of those days when a four-ounce fish seemed to me a monster. Like most chalk waters, the River Arle offers many varied opportunities. My favoured method is nymph fishing, which to a dry-fly purist may come as something of a shock, but to my mind the sight of a nice brown trout drifting off-station to intercept a nymph is one of the best sights in trout fishing. Like most chalk-stream fish, the Arle brown trout are not over-particular about which nymph to take—Pheasant Tail, Sawyer Bug, Leopard Nymph, Copper Nymph, even Leaded Shrimp are all good trout catchers. (In fact, with this short selection in his fly wallet, an angler should be able to catch trout from any venue he visits.)

On the Arle, I have favourite pools and bends—places where past trips have provided good fishing and where I have that added confidence to fish well. This is an important factor in successful fishing. To feel that a certain place or a certain fly will produce a fish is nine-tenths of success. There is one such pool where I know I can never fail to rise or catch a good brown trout. Essentially the Arle is a shallow river, but at one bend, where the main force of the current is deflected straight across to the other bank, the river has dug a deep, dark hole beneath a trailing willow. This is a place made for nymph fishing. In particular it is a shrimp-pattern lie and by careful casting I can place a shrimp on the lip of the hole. The trick of this place is to judge accurately the flow rate of the river, which can change from day to day. For this reason I carry a range of shrimp patterns in differing weights and colours. The tendency today seems to be for bright-coloured shrimps—vivid orange is a favourite colour—but to my mind this is unnatural. I prefer more natural colours—green, grey-brown and the light gold of the breeding shrimp. It is the gold colour that I choose for the dark hole, on the theory that it can easily be seen by the lurking trout—and, more important, that I can see it as it trundles into the water shadows. Many anglers watch the nylon leader for signs of a take. I am more fortunate—I possess the rare ability to see into water. For me a bite indication is a flash of fins or a slight oily displacement of water—both sure signs that a trout has intercepted my nymph.

The best brown trout that I have caught from this dark overhung pool weighed in at two pounds, two ounces—a minor fish by River Test or Itchen standards but one that I still recall with pleasure. I caught it on a day that was almost too bright for trout fishing, so bright in fact that the fish in more open water constantly refused both dry fly and nymph. As always I had walked the river slowly, saving my favourite pool for as long as possible. Coming at the end to the pool, I crept into casting position, making short false casts as I moved. The fly was a tiny Golden Shrimp which contained exactly the right

Dry fly fishing on the River Anton, one of the world's finest chalk streams.

amount of lead to allow instant penetration through the fast run of surface water. The first time the nymph worked through the pool I was certain I saw movement deep down and far back in the shadows. I decided to wait five minutes and work the pool a second time. I was not impatient. Five minutes by a river you love is five minutes in paradise—the bankside vegetation is alive with busy insects and the smell of freshly crushed water-mint is a heady aphrodisiac to the dedicated angler. When I was sure that I had rested the pool long enough I made my second cast, placing the shrimp directly on the lip of the pool. Seconds later I saw the quick flash of a broad tail. A rapidly wagging tail is a sure sign that a trout has a nymph well inside its mouth, so I struck hard. As the rod swept back I felt the solid impact of hook into hard flesh. The fish instantly bored down in a desperate attempt to gain sanctuary in the gnarled roots of the great willow, but by swinging the rod sideways I was able to slow it down and turn it away from the unseen root system. Next the fish turned downstream, bursting from the shadows into open and more shallow water; twice it jumped in a desperate attempt to shake the hook free. Finally it made a short, futile dash up-river before turning slowly on its side into the waiting net. It was in perfect physical condition, broad in the shoulder, its fins intact—the sort of fish that comes only a few times in any angler's life time.

Every chalk stream has its carrier streams, tiny neglected, often overgrown waterways that were once part of an intricate irrigation system used to govern the amount of water supplied to the water-meadows. These carrier stream often provide outstanding fishing, because big brown trout, tired of the competitive life of the main river, move into them to find plentiful food and freedom from the main-river rat race. These carrier fish are often overlooked, because most anglers prefer to fish the main and more open river. The little carrier streams are often exceptionally difficult to fish. Big trout living in a shallow, narrow water become cautious in the extreme. An untimely shadow or unwary footfall, even the flash of rod varnish, may cause instant panic.

Over the years I have made a practice of exploring these carriers and they have given me some exciting fishing. One such stream springs instantly to mind. Situated on a private estate, it runs between the Test and the Dever. Known locally as the 'Rainbow' stream, it is a narrow, shallow, carrier holding a limited head of large brown trout. Essentially it is dry-fly water—a stream in most places less than two feet deep that runs clear and clean over lush green weed interspersed with stretches of bright, pure gravel. The trout lie mostly beneath or close to the weed, each fish in a position that allows it to see food easily as it drifts down-river. The 'Rainbow' stream is a short-rod fishery: I use a one-piece six-foot split-cane wand that can throw a No. 5 line easily and accurately. To complement the casting action of this classic rod I use only the minutest of dry flies. My favourite pattern is an Iron-blue Dun—a fly which seems to appeal throughout the season. (I fish the stream at all times except during the mayfly hatch—mayfly imitations are at best bulky flies that overload the little one-piece rod.)

The fun of this stream is that it is necessary to get close to the feeding trout. The approach to a rising fish calls for great care—a mistimed cast can put the fish down for the day. I have lost count of how many fish I have frightened in this way, when the line or leader has dropped just that tiny bit hard.

To me, one fat brown trout from the carrier is worth four from the main river. Only once have I achieved a magical two brace from the carrier in a single day. It was one of these rare days when every fish in the carrier seemed to be on the rise. The month was July, the day overcast, and the stream thick with flowering water-weed. The low water level of summer and the heavy weed growth made casting extremely difficult. In many cases I had to drop the fly into an area less than two feet square. Any form of overcasting made the fly drag instantly. Accuracy was essential. Clumsy presentation put the first four fish down; after that I steadied off and began to fish well. My first fish was a plump well-spotted two pounder that had taken up a position below a bed of ranunculus—perfect from the trout's point of view, not so good from mine. Catching trout on carrier streams is very much like playing chess; the battle-ground has to be meticulously studied and options carefully considered. I decided on my approach and made my cast accordingly, the tiny dry fly landing a bare 12 inches beyond the clearly visible trout. The fish took the fly instantly and with total confidence and minutes later was in the net. During the next two hours I hooked three more fish; two I safely netted, the third broke free on an unseen obstruction.

Playing a trout on dry fly on a carrier of the River Test.

Right at the top end of the carrier was a hatch pool which created a miniature weir, which in turn had scoured out a deep, fast pool that normally held several good fish. It was the best pool of the stream and I had saved it until last. I reached it in late afternoon and sat and watched for signs of activity. Twice I caught the flash of broad primrose flanks as a fine trout turned to intercept a nymph. I like nymph fishing but I always fished the carrier only with a dry fly, a custom that I had no intention of changing. Life on a river is never static and within an hour the nymphs had given way to flies—tiny grey flies lifting and drifting as the mood took them. The fish were rising freely. Using again my Iron-blue Dun, I cast directly up to the throat of the hatch, planning to let the fly drift back to calmer water. But trout pay little attention to the plans of anglers—before the tiny fly had drifted a yard the fish rose heavily and the fly disappeared. I struck, and felt a vibrant drag on the rod tip as the fish surged round the pool. It was trapped in the pool; by walking out on the shallows I forestalled any attempt it might make to run downstream. Now with the cane rod in full battle curve I settled back to enjoy the battle. Constant rod pressure will wear down any fish. In less than five minutes the trout was starting to wallow; two minutes later it was in the net. It was a thickset five-pounder in perfect condition—a prize of a fish and a fitting end for a day on my favourite carrier stream.

Alas, the fishing rights on this estate have changed hands and the keeper is no longer allowed the odd day for friends, so these stretches of the Test and the Dever and their carrier streams are now just a memory.

Oddly enough my largest fly-caught brown trout also came from a Test carrier stream. For many years I fished on Broadlands Estate, taking a season rod on the trout stream, or 'ditch' as it is affectionately known. This tiny carrier was dug out and improved during Lord Louis Mountbatten's time. It has been lovingly cleared and landscaped and has become one of the most sought-after season-rod fisheries in southern England. The head keeper, Bernard Aldritch, maintains a careful stocking policy, introducing mostly rain-

bow trout but also the occasional brown trout and hybrid.

On the day I caught my big brown trout I had taken two brace of good rainbows and was looking for a bigger fish to round off the day. To this end, I switched to a weighted fly of my own invention, a pattern which, under the name of Dog Nobbler, has since become a world-wide success. I was working the fly back when I sensed rather than saw a shadow following it. I speeded up the retrieve and the shadow became a swiftly attacking fish. I watched fascinated as the fish gulped back the fly, but only as I raised the rod tip and set the hook did I appreciate that I had a brown trout, and a very big one. Big trout normally try to stay in their home territory, but this fish shot out of the pool and headed upstream into a narrow throat of water so overhung that to avoid snagging the line I was forced to thrust the rod tip under water. As I expected the combination of rod pressure and water pressure forced the trout back in the pool, where I was able to bully it into submission. Soon it was ready for netting and within minutes I was back at the fishing hut for the official weighing-in ceremony.

The fish had not a blemish on its body, not a fin out of place. Clearly it was not a stock fish; it was probably one that had found its way by accident into the carrier and had remained to live and grow on a diet of small trout and minnows. It weighed seven and a quarter pounds. It was a beautiful fish.

10
Tuna

Fighting the Blue Fin and Big Eye

My boyhood reading had included numberless stories about tuna and tuna fishing—stories from the icy North Sea where giant blue fin harried the herring shoals, from Long Island, Nova Scotia, the Bahamas and Madeira; stories of epic battles, broken rods, seized reels and strong lines snapped like cotton. So when, childhood long behind me, I was invited to fish tuna off Madeira I jumped at the chance. This was my introduction to the island and I gaped tourist-like at the mountains above Funchal, at the local ox carts and at the variety of flowers, fruit and fish in the town market. I spent my first two days sightseeing, travelling around the island from the arid area round Machico up through cloud-cloaked mountains to the lovely greenery of Santana,

Author with a fine Atlantic big eye tuna. An 80 lb or 130 lb class IGFA rod should be used in the deep water of the Atlantic. In the USA and Canada, where the depth is not as great, lighter tackle can be used.

Big eye tuna lashed to the side of a boat.

before moving on to the wild and rugged coastline of the north. I was struck by the friendliness of the local people. Whenever I stopped anywhere near habitation someone would appear within seconds with a jug of the strong, almost black, local wine.

Such was the hospitality that it was probably just as well that on the third day I started fishing. The Madeira Tourist Office had kindly loaned me their lovely boat *Altair*, a local-built game-fishing machine that had the lines of a racehorse. I had brought two sets of my own tackle and the boat carried two more outfits that I could use. One of these was a massive, obviously well-used, Hardy game rod, built to the highest of specifications. It was matched by a monster Ocean City multiplier, a 16-0 giant that looked capable of taming any tuna alive. The first day was a blank. For hour after hour we trolled a zig-

Sea birds feeding over bait fish are an sign that tuna are in the area, or soon will be.

zag beat that took us out for over twenty miles. The November sunshine was warm and bright and the air like crystal. Not a fish broke the mirror-like surface of the ocean, although the skipper assured me that tuna were in the area—he thought they had gone deep following the shoals of bait fish. Nonetheless we kept at it. It is always, on this sort of expedition, a mistake to relax, because a strike can occur at any time. We called it a day only when darkness fell, heading back then to a welcome shower, a drink and a much-needed meal. On day two we tried, with equal lack of success, in the vicinity of Pont San Lourenco lighthouse, a noted tuna-feeding area.

The third day dawned bright and clear, without the slightest breath of wind to ruffle the untroubled surface of the ocean. By noon the sun was blisteringly hot. We still had not sighted a fish. Then, at about half past one, I heard the rigger pin snap out and the Ocean City reel start to snarl as a big fish headed down into deep water. 'Tuna!' the skipper shouted, 'a blue fin, maybe 500 kilos.' The possible weight of the fish was not at the time my most immediate concern; I was struggling to control the wildly bucking rod while I climbed into the simple wooden fighting chair. Once in and settled, I applied addi-

The mate of a Pescatur boat holds a newly gaffed big eye, with the colours still fresh—these quickly turn to grey. The fish is typical of an early season tuna.

Atlantic blue fin tuna next to a blue shark, taken off the coast of the Algarve, Portugal.

Boating a big eye tuna taken off the Azores.

178

red glass eye

feathers

chromed lead

tional pressure in the hope of slowing the fish down, but the fish was too intent on finding the shelter of black water far below our keel even to notice my efforts. But I had well over 1,000 yards of 130-class dacron line on the reel and felt able to take anything the fish could hand out. So it was a shock when I suddenly realized that the reel would soon be empty of line. I could not believe the ease with which the fish emptied that reel; yard after yard vanished from the great drum, exposing more and more of the chromed spool as the fish sped on. All too soon I could see that there was less than 50 yards left. But then, unbelievably and inexplicably, the fish stopped. There were only a few

Japanese feather lures are very successful as bait for both big eye and blue fin tuna. It helps to match the 'feather' colour to the colour of bait fish present in the feeding area. These lures, especially when yellow, are also good for barracuda

Big eye tuna taken on a Japanese feather. Big eye fight harder and faster than blue fin tuna.

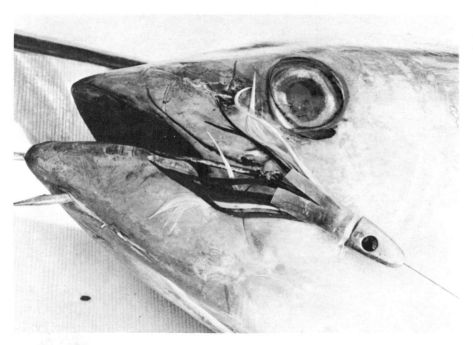

Funchal, Madeira. Author with a big eye tuna.

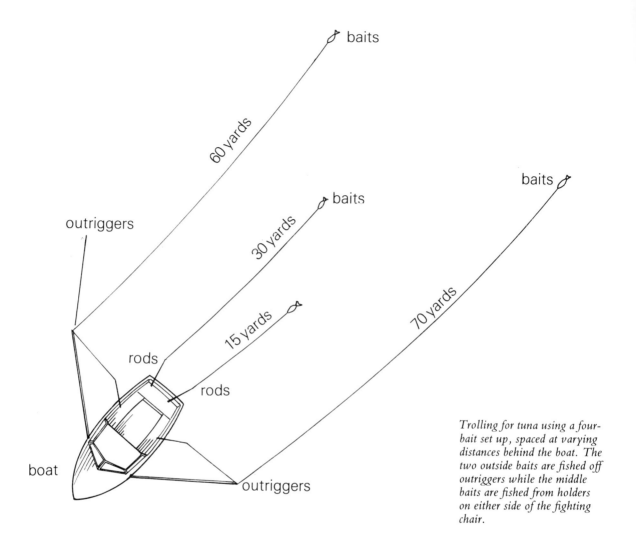

baits

baits

baits

60 yards

30 yards

15 yards

70 yards

outriggers

rods

rods

boat

outriggers

Trolling for tuna using a four-bait set up, spaced at varying distances behind the boat. The two outside baits are fished off outriggers while the middle baits are fished from holders on either side of the fighting chair.

short turns of line left on the spool; had the fish run a fraction further it would have reached the end of the line and smashed the reel knot. I now had a chance to start working the fish back towards the surface. With all the line out, I was naturally determined to gain as much as possible before the fish decided to run again. Pumping a big tuna up from deep water is a hard, slogging operation— the sheer bulk of the fish makes it difficult to shift—and it took over an hour to half-fill the reel spool. During this hour the fish simply used its body as a drogue, hanging like a dead weight, I knew it was still alive only because it occasionally shook its head. This was puzzling, but I was well into the rhythm of things and felt confident of beating the fish providing no accidents occurred. The reel spool continued to fill. Then, without warning, the rod was almost

Angler with big eye tuna, Madeira.

ripped from my hands as the fish turned and ran back into deep water at desperate speed. This time I applied more rod pressure in an attempt to slow the fish down. Unfortunately, this was more than the old and much-used Hardy rod could stand—with over 600 yards of line out it broke at a point about 15 inches from the tip. But I had enough rod left still to apply reasonable leverage and the battle continued. The fish settled again, content once more to lie almost inert in the dark water. Again I started the long pump-and-wind action necessary to bring it up from the depths. Once more it lifted easily, rising steadily towards the surface. With less than 100 yards of line to take in I was certain I had the fish finished. The tuna, though, had other ideas. One second it was allowing itself to be led like a dog, the next it was galvanized into action, plunging once more into the depths. The violence of its dive ripped all the rings from the remaining length of rod. To this day I have no idea just what happened, but I assume that a loop of line jammed in the rings. For whatever reason, I was left with only a reel and a splintered stick in my hands and I was totally out of the fight. The boat crew managed to handline a very tired monster tuna to the surface, where the hook simply fell out of its jaw. In seconds the huge fish had finned its way out of sight.

Naturally, the loss of this fish made me feel that my luck was very definitely out. Fortunately, however, I took two large big eye tuna the next day. Big eye tuna never reach the great weights attained by the mighty blue fin, but these fish weighed in at over 200 pounds, which was more than respectable.

For me, blue fin tuna have always presented a problem. I have caught several medium-weight fish, of 400 to 500 pounds, but the big 800-pounders have managed to elude me. Once, fishing in the Bahamas, I hooked a huge blue fin that took a trolled bait in comparatively shallow water close to the 100-fathom drop-off. I should explain that the trick with giant tuna is to keep them in shallow areas where they cannot dive. This confuses them to such an extent that they can often be boated in a remarkably short time. Once in deep water the same fish may take hours to bring to the boat. This fish snatched at a gaudy lure, hooked itself up and hightailed it for the open sea. Within 200 yards it was out into deep water and heading down at high speed. When our skipper positioned the boat directly above it I estimated that it had taken nearly 300 yards of line. This meant two things—firstly, that I was in for a hard brutal battle and, second, that I would be lucky to get the fish up in one piece. A frantically fighting tuna puts out tremendous vibrations, which attract sharks in search of an easy meal. I slogged it out trying to raise the fish as quickly as possible, but as fast as I gained line the fish took it back. It was the sort of ding-dong battle that tuna specialize in. It lasted for two hours, then I felt a hard bump on the line and knew that the first shark had struck the still-fighting tuna. Within minutes the bumping motion increased and soon the fish stopped fighting altogether. I felt sick, not at losing the fish but at the manner of its death. Tethered by my line, the great ocean wanderer was easy game for any marauding shark pack. Winding became easier as the shark carved weight from the tuna's corpse. Soon the remnants of the fish were in sight, mangled and destroyed. Two big tiger sharks and a huge hammerhead followed the mutilated fish right up to the boat; when we opened the tuna door in the boat's transom they fought to follow the tuna inboard. Bahamian boat crews

A massive blue fin tuna being weighed at Walker's Cay. Blue fin tuna can reach weights of 1,000 lb or more. Kona Head lures should be all black, or occasionally green and yellow.

have no love for shark and as the fish jostled to gain entry the steady thwack of baseball clubs meeting sharks' heads echoed round the boat. Later the remains of the tuna weighed in at 510 pounds.

Big tuna are probably the hardest fish of all to bring to the boat. American anglers would probably disagree, but that is because most of their fish are taken in extremely shallow water. Once hooked, a tuna invariably heads straight for the sea bed and when it reaches the bottom it seems to lose heart so that it can be boated quickly and easily. Off the traditional North American tuna ports the water is often less than 100 feet deep. Off the Azores or Madeira a tuna may take a bait over hundreds of fathoms of water and that is when it comes into its own. I have seen many marathon battles with tuna that have sounded to extreme depths and fought for six or eight hours. It takes a special breed of angler to fight big tuna over this period of time. It is a dour and bitter struggle and the angler has to work flat out to raise the fish. Despite the muscle-tearing exertions of such a battle, the final sighting of a vast tuna more than makes up for the misery involved. Since my first encounter with blue fin I have hooked many hefty specimens. Most of them have been taken in deep water.

For sheer sport the smaller tuna provide the best fishing. A good-sized big eye tuna or a heavy yellowfin takes some beating. Both fish fight hard and fast, often putting up a battle far in excess of their comparatively light weights. Big eye tuna are the best fun of all—they run in huge packs and when you

Author with big eye tuna, San Miguel.

find one you usually find many. On a number of occasions I have seen four
hooked up at the same time, a situation which can rapidly lead to chaos.
Crossed and broken lines are common as each fish hits the bait and dives
instantly for deep water. Normally when big eye tuna are plentiful it pays to
dispense with the four-rod system and use just two lures. This can save losing
baits, fish and expensive line.

When tuna are surface feeding in this way I prefer to dispense with expensive Kona Head lures and use lead-headed Japanese feathers, which catch well,
but are comparatively inexpensive. I remember trolling one such bait for a
whole day without success on the south side of Madeira. Tuna had been in the
area on the previous day, but now the ocean seemed devoid of life. By late
afternoon we decided to give it best and head back to Funchal, trolling baits as
we went. The strike took us all by surprise. By the splash, and the way the fish
instantly dived, I assumed it to be a tuna. It fought a deep, hard battle for
thirty minutes and then began to give ground. Slowly I was able to gain line

until the fish was within 50 yards of the surface, when I increased rod and drag pressure, intent on finishing the fight as quickly as possible. Moments later a monster shark surfaced in a flurry of white water. Exact identification was impossible, but from its vast size and its pale slate-white colour we all assumed it to be a great white. I shall always remember the vast size of its tail and the mountain of white water that shot skywards as it crash-dived out of sight again. The boat's skipper took one look at it and pronounced it a record. He also said that in his opinion it was foul-hooked. I agreed with him on both counts. The fish looked over 16 feet long and from the angle of the line I guessed it to be hooked close to the mouth. Nonetheless, rather than give up and cut the line I decided to continue the battle. I suppose I had some crazy idea of eventually wearing the fish down. What I could not understand was its fight style; everything about it was tuna-like, yet I had seen it clearly and knew it to be a shark. During the next two hours I had the fish on the surface half-a-dozen times and on each occasion saw it quite clearly as a shark. The rod had the then common cork hand grips and I put so much pressure on the fish that the corks began to split. The rough edges of broken cork then started to grind into my hands, forming massive blisters which then chaffed through, exposing raw flesh. I was not aware of pain at the time, although I knew my hands were in bad shape; the adrenalin was running and I felt good enough to stay with the fish.

Finally I had the trace out of the water and, as the skipper grasped the wire, we were drenched by a huge flailing tail. The mate gaffed deep into the heart of the disturbance and heaved—and a 300-pound tuna catapulted out of the water practically into the boat. The shark had obviously stayed with the tuna hoping for an easy meal. The tuna, terrified out of its mind, had fought twice as hard to try and avoid the monster's jaws, I had won the battle but had paid the price; the flesh was practically torn from my hands. When I climbed from the fighting chair I saw for the first time twin pools of blood on the deck—formed by blood running down my forearms to drip off my elbows. For a month afterwards my hands needed constant medical attention; I was unable to pick up the smallest item and fishing was totally out of the question. Tuna under normal circumstances are tough fighters. With a huge shark after them their power can be totally unbelievable.

When I now read the old accounts of pioneer days at Avalon and Catalina I marvel at the strength and determination of those early tuna fishermen. By modern standards their tackle was crude and totally insufficient for the job on hand. But those early American anglers achieved heroic results, results which have led to many major developments in equipment and techniques. However, even with the best tackle a big tuna is a tough proposition. I would rate it one of the toughest fish on earth.

Index